D0228049

*Catherine
Bramwell-Booth*
LETTERS

Affectionately and loyally
to my Father and General

Catherine Bramwell-Booth

LETTERS

A twentieth-century spiritual classic
Introduced by MARY BATCHELOR

A LION PAPERBACK
Tring · Batavia · Sydney

Letters was first published in book form
under the title *Messages to the Messengers*
issued by Salvationist Publishing and
Supplies Ltd, London, being letters to
former cadets by Catherine Bramwell-Booth
reprinted from *The Officer*

Copyright © 1921 Catherine Bramwell-Booth

Published by
Lion Publishing plc
Icknield Way, Tring, Herts, England
ISBN 0 7459 1173 0
Albatross Books Pty Ltd
PO Box 320, Sutherland, NSW 2232, Australia
ISBN 0 86760 826 9

New edition with introduction and notes 1986

British Library Cataloguing in Publication Data
Bramwell-Booth, Catherine
    Catherine Bramwell-Booth: letters.—
    New ed., with introduction and notes.
    1. Bramwell-Booth, Catherine   2. Salvation-
    ists—Great Britain—Biography
    I. Title   II. Batchelor, Mary
    III. Bramwell-Booth, Catherine. Messages
    to the messengers
    267' .15' 0924   BX97L3.B84/
    ISBN 0 7459 1173 0

Printed in Great Britain
by Richard Clay (The Chaucer Press) Ltd,
Bungay, Suffolk

CONTENTS

CONTENTS

Introduction

CATHERINE BRAMWELL-BOOTH was born in 1883, the eldest child of Bramwell and Florence Booth and first grandchild of William and Catherine, founders of The Salvation Army. Bramwell, who became the movement's second General, or leader, had also been involved with the beginnings of The Army and was his father's right-hand man, working unremittingly for what father and son referred to affectionately as the 'Concern'.

Catherine and her six sisters and brothers grew up in a world bounded by The Salvation Army, but they loved it despite the heavy demands that it made on both their parents. They had an idyllically happy childhood and all chose to enter The Army as full-time officers. Catherine left home for officer training when she was nineteen and by the time she was twenty-one ran a local Army corps, or church, as its minister, with a woman lieutenant (or 'curate') to help her. Her duties included taking the regular services, evangelistic preaching in and out of doors, meeting social needs and visiting and caring for her local 'soldiers' or church members.

It was the beginning of a long career for The Army – and for Christ – lasting far beyond official retirement age to her one hundredth birthday, when she became a public figure through her appearances on television.

After experience in the field she was appointed at twenty-four to the staff of the Training Garrison, as it was then called, in Clapton, London, where she remained for the next ten years. Students, or cadets, came to the college from every walk of life. Some could not read or write when they arrived and all were chosen for their spiritual rather than their intellectual potential.

Catherine taught the 'women's side' in lectures and classes, in a course that combined, in true Army fashion, spiritual wisdom and sound common sense. The cadets were reminded that The Army's aim was to save souls and to love men and women for Christ.

As well as teaching classes, Catherine took infinite pains to gain the confidence of every one of her cadets and to give them opportunity to share their anxieties and problems with her. It is not surprising that when they, in turn, were fully-fledged officers in the field, they wrote to 'Major Catherine' with their worries and concerns. Bramwell Booth suggested that instead of replying to each girl individually, Catherine should publish one letter a month in a current Army magazine called *The Officer*. The officer for whom the letter was specifically intended was told about its publication beforehand, but initials were changed so that no one else would guess her identity.

In 1921 The Salvation Army published the collected letters in a book, called *Messages to the Messengers*, now long since out of print.

The letters are written both from the head and from the heart. Catherine's considerable intellect, shrewd common sense, honesty and personal experience were all brought to bear on the problems raised. Her answers are sometimes comforting, sometimes uncomfortably probing and challenging, but always right on target. Catherine did not easily bare her soul. A contemporary Army account says that 'her inner life—the struggles of her soul—is sacred to herself, except in so far as its lessons help others'. In this book she shares her own rich spiritual and practical experience with her readers.

The book is highly relevant not only to Salvationists but also to every Christian engaged both in personal spiritual battle and in trying to take the gospel of Jesus Christ 'behind enemy lines'. It is, indeed, a spiritual classic, now within reach of the whole Christian world.

MARY BATCHELOR

Preface

THE LETTERS gathered in this small volume were written whilst I was an officer at the International Training Garrison, London. That they might ever appear in book form happily did not occur to me or they would, I think, not have been written.

When my father suggested that I should write a monthly letter in 'The Officer', he convinced me that it would help many of the younger officers. The hope of doing this inspired a courage which triumphed over fears awakened by the prospect of editors and print; and thinking only of those whom I longed to help, I wrote down what I wanted to say to them. The writing was, I thought, only an ephemeral expression of my thoughts and desires for those souls: the most I hoped was that some helpful recollection of the message might remain, as the memory of wild flowers lingers after the blossoms have faded. The attempt to preserve these jottings between two covers may prove as unsatisfactory as pressing a daisy in a copy-book! They were none of them intended for such preservation, but rather to bloom in their short day and disappear.

Others than those to whom I wrote them received the messages, and they, as well as many of my 'children' of Clapton, want to look at them again. And so, hoping some may be helped in a moment of need, I welcome the opportunity of sending out the little volume, not as the ripened fruit, but rather as a handful of wild flowers of thought, hastily gathered, to cheer and counsel my 'children'.

From one line of battle to another these messages went. You who stand in the firing line will not be astonished that they were often written during the small hours of the morning, when a swiftly passing silence fell upon the Clapton streets, and one could be sure of an uninterrupted spell, unless indeed the night watchman blundered in to put out the light. Some I wrote piecemeal in moments snatched from the over-crowded hours of those dear Training Garrison days. Those who know the glorious rush of our Salvation Army War will not expect to find in these pages the perfection which takes time, but will, I hope, recognize here and there the touch which love can give in the twinkling of an eye.

To the children of 'Clapton' and its precincts, I say again God-speed! Brave young hearts, defy the years! Press on with the duties of the Kingdom; march with songs upon yours lips, with patience, and, if the need call, with tears, but ever without halting, until we march through the Gates into the City. And until then, be ever looking unto Jesus—

Love Him, and trust Him, follow Him with pains,
　　Not easily—the grace is for the strife;
And whatsoever trial He may lay
　　Upon thee, trust Him through it, and give thanks;
And when thy heart is heavy think on Him;
　　And when thy need is greatest call on Him.
Hold fast God's promise, and remember this—
　　Christ will not fail thee.

CATHERINE BOOTH
BARNET, 14 FEBRUARY 1921

1
TO ONE IN A SMALL COUNTRY TOWN

My Dear W____,

I have thought so much of you since I saw you; and, after your graphic description, I can picture you in your little town, where I pray God may so help you, that, at least so far as sinners, sufferers, and little children are concerned, you may soon be the best-loved person in the place.

I have been thinking over all you told me, and I do realize that you have very real difficulties. The slow-going country people, with their prejudice against innovations, their willingness to receive *you*, and their unwillingness to receive *God*; the way they come in and listen; and the way, Sunday after Sunday, they go out and reject, must, I know, severely test your faith. But do not be discouraged, even if you work long with only small results. Towns such as X—— are common enough, and we must not give up because the devil is learning to oppose us more successfully with indifference than by stirring people up to persecute.

We must learn to attack in a new way, if the old ways produce little result. The enemy's tactics change, and so must ours. So often the fight we imagined would be the fiercest does not face us; instead, we are met by the enemy on unexpected ground, and find ourselves taken by surprise.

Now you must be as determined to win under present circumstances as you would have been had the devil come in the way for which you were prepared. Because the self-denial to which you are called is not just the kind you thought it would be, don't despise it. *Do not make the mistake of wanting to choose how you shall suffer!* You are ready to suffer, I know: indeed, I believe you would do so gladly; but the fact is, you have not yet recognized that the circumstances of the moment give you the opportunity you covet.

If you were being subjected to a form of outward persecution—to ridicule in the streets and to violence in the meetings—you would, as you say, glory in it. But don't you see, that to accept the criticisms of your soldiers and the stony indifference of the sinners, is really just as truly an opportunity to triumph? Perhaps even a better; because to a nature like yours, it means a bigger victory to be kind and to *feel* kind towards folk who run you down behind your back, than to smile in return for a rotten tomato during the open-air!

You must come to a place in your heart's experience where you *accept today's opportunity* as that in which you can best prove your love to God and to souls; whether it be just in the way you had planned and hoped or not.

Ambition for big things in the service of God is good— and, you know, I only wish more among you girls aimed high—but *an ambition that makes you look slightingly on the possibilities now in your hands will defeat its own ends.* Our mountains are only reached step by step from the valley.

My prayer for you is not so much that God may give you the joy of a sweeping success in X—— as that He may give you eyes to see the value of the 'little' chance within your reach.

Remember the Lord's own similitude: 'The Kingdom of Heaven is like to a grain of mustard seed.' Sow the grain, even if it be only the grain of a kindly word to the cranky soldier, or the kissing of some grubby little kiddy, or the tear shed in secret, or the effort in the open-air on a wet night; for out of such seeds springs up the Kingdom of Heaven in the hearts of men.

Do believe it! It is not for you and me to be deciding what shall prosper—whether this or that. *Our* business is to do the sowing well.

My own experience teaches me more and more that when we are wholly God's, *all we do* can be made an offering worthy of His acceptance. You remember the song of the College days:

> All I think or speak or do,
> Is one great sacrifice.

This realization that no detail of my private or public life is too small to be done 'as unto the Lord', has brought such comfort, especially in the doing of irksome things, the cost of doing which no one around me understood or appreciated. The little sacrifice is often so much harder to make for that reason—we feel that others often cannot justly measure the price we paid. But the Lord always can, and values it accordingly.

Do banish for ever the thought that either God or the world is waiting to see you prove your love by some big sacrifice or outwardly heroic service. Opportunities for such are rare, but the chance to prove our devotion in common everyday things belongs to us all. The world today, perhaps more than ever before, needs apostles of the commonplace, the living of the life of Jesus in the ordinary insignificances that go to make up an average day; and the Lord still honours the servant who is faithful 'in that which is least'.

Start out tomorrow with this thought uppermost. When you forgo your own preference about some aggravating little thing in the quarters, realize that *that* is offered to the Lord. When your visiting brings you face to face with the people's indifference, and your soul shrinks from their vulgar gossip, deal with them patiently, faithfully, believingly, in His name. Even asking for the collection, or smoothing down old Brother J___ for the ninety-ninth time; *all*, day after day, if truly done for Christ, goes to make your 'sacrifice complete'.

I understand what you feel when you speak of the ungratefulness of your own people—how they seem to take what you do as a matter of course. But does not that bring us back to the same point? If all is being done *for God*, then we shall not be hurt by *their* lack of gratitude.

For you, my dear W___, as for me, the secret of our joy is that we find it in *Christ*. If this is so, we shall not be cast down or silenced when we fail to see the results we hoped for in our work, or the response we expected from those we serve, for He will be our 'exceeding great reward'.

Believing this, you can make the dullest place a heavenly place, and you will realize more and more the presence of the Lord Himself. Only make sure that you go often enough where He most longs to lead You—to the public-house, to the homes of the people, to any and every place within your reach where you may find the sinner and the sufferer, those who, either in body or in soul, are lame or halt or blind. Try doing what, perhaps, you have not done since you were a cadet, *visit the public-houses*, in addition to going with the papers on Saturday night. Be amongst the people 'as one that serveth', and before you dream of it you may find yourself amongst them as 'one that reigneth'.

I believe for you! God will use you in X___, in spite of its wickedness, in spite of its indifference, and in spite of the way others may have failed. In *you* He will manifest His Son, and the devil shall be defeated 'again and again'. But remember, these big results have their beginnings in 'that which is least'.

Yours, to serve

2
ON KEEPING FIRST
THINGS FIRST

FEBRUARY 1914

Dear S____,

You do not know what a joy it is to me to have such good news of you; to hear not only that the corps is doing well, but that you are revelling in it all. I have prayed for you in past days that you might feel your work for souls to be not only your duty, but your *joy*. Thank God, He is so enlarging your heart that only such joy can fill it.

There are many things I would like to write to you, and heaps of questions I want to ask, but neither you nor I have time. If I could pop down and see you 'at it', I would find a talk over a fire a much more satisfying thing than a letter. But it cannot be.

Be wise. Take proper care. Get your sleep and food regularly; for, in order to get the most done, you must go to work in the best way, even with regard to the body.

Beware of spending too large a proportion of your time and strength on matters of only secondary importance. Learn to distinguish what is vital from what is merely incidental; and, above all, resolve by God's help at all cost to *keep first things first*.

Foremost among the first is the welfare of your own soul. As is the state of the fire to the steam-engine, so is the condition of your soul to your work. A neglected fire means less steam, and after a bit, failure to move the train. A neglected soul means less strength, and after a bit, a fainting under the burden of the day.

As Army officers we have always—at least I have found it so—more to do than time in which to do it. The devil knows this, and persistently attempts to thrust the work we love between us and the Source of our strength. Unless, therefore, the care of your soul is to you the *first* care, and is jealously guarded by you as such, the devil will succeed in putting into that first place the work itself; later, success at the expense of good work; and, at last, purely selfish interest will reign in the once sanctified soul.

It cannot be denied that there is a frightful possibility of being engaged in God's work, prophesying in His name, casting out devils, doing many wonderful works, and yet *not* to be doing the will of God in our own hearts. Surely, above every fear—driving into the background the fear of failure, the fear of slander, and the fear of man—should be the fear lest, 'when I have preached to others, I myself should be a castaway.' I do beg you to be careful that no other desire take the place of that whole-souled determination to *be* what God wants.

To compromise often looks so reasonable; it seems such a little thing to consider for once how some action will affect your popularity, instead of considering first how it will affect your soul. It is so easy to step aside from what is strictly and wholly true and Christlike for the sake of temporary gain or advancement. A small step aside widens to a gulf when you want to get back; and these are the things that separate the soul from the Saviour, who said of Himself, 'I am the truth', and to whose followers it was written, 'If any man have not the Spirit of Christ, he is none of His.'

There is much I could write as to this, but I will only add these few words of advice. Exercise yourself continually in whatever special means of grace you may have found helpful.

Prayer. Do you keep up the 'half-hour'? Plan for it. I think I told you once that when I was in the field I found it best to arrange so that lieutenant and I had a different time. This meant we were not interrupted by any one who came to the door. One day I had mine immediately after breakfast, while lieutenant washed up and started to prepare dinner; and that day lieutenant had hers directly after dinner, while I washed up and laid tea. The next day vice versa. When you cannot get the whole half-hour at one time, plan for two quarters; *but get it!* It may mean leaving undone something you meant to do, but it will also mean that all you do will be better done.

Reading. You have not much opportunity for receiving help from meetings. As an FO you are always giving and seldom getting; but I would say, make the very most of the chances you *do* have. Go to the officers' meetings with your heart prepared, for we often miss what God has made ready because the vessel is not open to receive.

Now, wise reading will do much to make up for this lack. Read the Bible, of course. Take it in more than a mouthful at a time, and not only when you want it just to give out again. Read it, seeking for the personal application of what you read. Have always one helpful book at hand, or if possible, two; so that if you do not feel inclined for one, you can read the other.

It is amazing how much you can read in a little time. I learned while I was in the field to read in snatches, and I have been thankful ever since. You are a captain, so can make your own plans. Why not decide to read at one meal in the day? Let each have a book. You get plenty of occasions to talk, and would not, I think, miss this opportunity for conversation.

When visiting means a long walk into the country, have a book with you, and take it in turns to read aloud. This should be a book kept to read together on such occasions. You will also find that a chapter the last thing at night helps to drive out the petty worries of the day, besides sending you to sleep with a helpful thought in mind.

I would say never read fiction, except when on furlough, and then choose it wisely. There is so much that is helpful, soul-nourishing, and heart-inspiring in the experiences, thoughts, and doings of real men and women, that the Salvation Army officer is the last person who in the midst of his work should live in an imaginary world.

Devotional intercourse. Cultivate this. Make prayer together in the quarters a real force. Seize the opportunity for conversation on spiritual things whenever you are in the company of comrades. Some of my richest blessings have come to me in this manner. Chats by the wayside, or over the meal-table, or during a chance visit, when the talk was finished up by prayer together—these have been means God has used to water my heart's thirsty ground.

Feed the flock. Paul placed the care of the flock next to the care of our own souls: 'Take heed therefore unto yourselves, and to all the flock, over the which the Holy Ghost hath made you overseers, to feed the church of God.' Surely, caring for the flock is amongst the *first things* for us.

How shall it be said to glorify your Lord, if the numbers increase and the band improve and your new songsters develop, unless souls are fed; unless under your ministrations they grow strong in the Lord? Make them *feel* that their souls' welfare is your first consideration. Inquire about their experience as being more important to you than anything else.

We grieve over the number of backsliders to be found in many corps; but I feel afraid when I think of the explanation that might be given from Heaven as to *why* they backslide. Had the shepherd of the flock cared enough for their souls to reprove, to advise, to inquire, they might have been of us still.

To guard and strengthen the spiritual life of our people should be our aim in all we do for them: the end of all the means we use. Many means are used, duties gather in connexion with those means; but do not allow the means to loom up as more important than the end. That would be like putting the care of the clothes before the care of the child, or like a captain I heard of who spent three hours repairing the curtains for the front room, but had no time for house-to-house visitation. Tidy quarters are, no doubt, a means to an end, but they are not that end. We must keep the end in view always.

Better, therefore, to go and fetch a convert to the meeting, even if you do less well in your talk, than to prepare the most careful address and not have him there to hear it. Better deal faithfully with a soul when visiting, and lose your tea, than, by staying to tea and chat, miss the opportunity for helping that soul. Make it impossible for any of your people to say of you what a soldier once said to me: 'The officers never come to my house unless to call for money or to get a meal.'

Better finish up on Sunday night with prayer and words of advice and encouragement, sending the soldiers and converts away inspired by the influences of the last fifteen minutes, even if you *are* five shillings and eleven pence half-penny short in collections for the day. Better a loss financially than a 'wind up' that helps the finances up, but brings the spiritual temperature down.

Yours, dear S——, is soul work—your own soul—the soul of the soldier—the soul of the sinner. God is helping you. Oh, may He teach you more fully that in work for Him the spiritual must be always before the material, the eternal before the temporal, the things not seen before the things which are seen!

Yours, to serve

3

TO ONE MISJUDGED

My Dear F____,

I am short of time (rather more so than usual), and am not able to write you as fully as I should like. But I just want to say that I *do* sympathize with you. I know something of how bitter a thing a seemingly unjust judgment of one's work can be; but, believe me, like some other bitter things, it may bring forth sweetness for you in God's good providence.

I do not want to sermonize, or to say anything that looks like an attempt to explain away the difficulty; for I know that even if I succeeded to my own satisfaction, I should not to yours. Words have no power to change facts, and you are face to face with certain facts at this moment that I know well are painful and discouraging. But do not consider the question as though there were only one side to it.

Remember, *other people's estimate of your work cannot change its quality.* Pronouncing good work bad does not make it bad; nor does calling bad work good make it good; nor have reports on paper, favourable or unfavourable, power to add to or take away one iota of accomplished good. The first question for you, about all your work, must be: Is it good in God's sight? In other words, whether my talents were two or fifty, did I do my best? Your *best* will be valued in Heaven because it *is* your best. 'She hath done what she could,' Jesus said on one of the rare occasions when He expressed His approbation of an individual act. And what words could have expressed higher praise?

Some one has written: 'In whatever offerings we may now see reason to present unto God, a condition of their acceptableness will be that they should be the best of their kind.' Do all you can, do the best you can, keep on doing it, and what credit you get, or even whether you get justice, will be of small importance.

Remember, further, *good work* has constantly received adverse judgments. Sometimes this comes as a result of a mistaken view; sometimes with evil intent on the part of those who judge. All of us who are working for God must expect that there will be times when we shall suffer as a result of one or the other. Is the servant above his Lord? Was not He blamed without a cause? Was not He misunderstood? Was not His good evil spoken of, and His work misrepresented? 'Beloved, think it not strange concerning the fiery trial which is to try you, as though some strange thing happened unto you. But rejoice inasmuch as ye are partakers of Christ's sufferings.' There is an experience possible to you and me. Paul testifies to it when he says: 'With me it is a very small thing that I should be judged of you, or of man's judgment . . . but He that judgeth me is the Lord.'

To leave our reputation with regard to our work in God's hands, is a hard lesson for some of us; and yet there can be no true and lasting peace of heart until we can say with Isaiah: 'My judgment is with the Lord, and my work with my God.'

Last, but not least, be sure that there is something for you to learn in this that will be a help in the future. You are not to blame to the extent ____ says; yet probably there are some points in which you could have done better. Do not refuse to admit this. One of the truest evidences of real wisdom is the ability to see our mistakes. To fail to do this puts you on the way to join the folk who think themselves martyrs, when other folk can only think them fools. You will come through. My advice is to leave the matter, then come back to it, and go carefully through all the circumstances, deciding with an impartial mind where and how you can improve, and resolving by the Lord's help that the past shall help the future.

Remember that the failure of today is, to the sanctified soul, but the seed of tomorrow's victory. The valley of humiliation prepares us for the victory over Apollyon. But all results depend on the spirit in which you meet things. Resentment and despondency allowed now may rob you of blessing, and leave you only wounded in spirit and weaker in soul for the experience; but humility and faith will bring you through richer in knowledge and stronger in grace.

Fight the battle out to the finish on your knees. Triumph in *spirit*, and you will triumph indeed. We still sing at the 'ten minutes':

> Give them trust that brings the triumph
>   When defeat seems strangely near!
> Give them faith that changes fighting
>   Into victory's ringing cheer!
> Faith triumphant, knowing not defeat nor fear!

And, thinking of you, my heart says, 'Amen!'

Yours, to serve you

4

APPOINTMENTS

My Dear J____,

How can you expect anything decent in the shape of a letter in these days? Do you remember what time of the year it is at the College? For whether it comes in summer or winter, spring or autumn, commissioning time is the same. And this is commissioning time. The realization of its approach has been dawning on me since one of the girls announced at the Home Lodge breakfast table, that it was 'only fourteen weeks to commissioning'! Now they are counting the hours!

These closing days make me sometimes sad, sometimes happy. Happy mostly when I think of those of you who are bravely in the fighting line. But there is real sorrow when I seem to see the faces of those who are no longer 'of us'. On the whole, it is a sad time in the old place. I hate seeing girls go just as much as I did when *you* went. Anyway, nearly as much!

Have you forgotten those last days? There are some things it always does us good to remember now and then—things that belong to the eternities of our lives; but how strangely we find our minds clinging to these memories of little things that belong only to their own day! Do *you* find mixed up with your recollections of the Colonel's words of burning exhortations in the last side classes, various scraps of instruction as to packing and tying on of labels? And do you remember speculating as to who were to be the new sergeants? Well, it is all going on as usual—the fitting on of new uniforms, the casting off of ancient goods. Every sound and sight tells me commissioning is coming, and at night I can hardly sleep for thinking over the appointments.

Covenant day comes, and we know the end is at hand, for in some ways the end *is* on that day. Do you remember it your session? The subdued excitement, the tremblings of heart, and the brigade officers mysteriously maneuvring the seating arrangements? I do! It was indeed a 'spiritual' day, but there was something special about that night meeting. I remember what we sang after those moments of prayer, with hands uplifted and faces turned to Heaven. I opened my eyes to look at you all. Oh, the ache of such moments! The conflict between hope and fear for some; for all, that insistent faith that seems to drink up even bodily strength in the intensity of its yearning. I prayed for you then with tears, that 'thy faith fail not.'

I do not think you realized then what it meant to the officers to see you coming up to that moment. I wonder if, now that you know something of what it is to 'watch for souls', you understand better? In the lecture hall on such days I seem sometimes to see not only the faces that *are* there, but those that once *were* there. And oh, how I long that, though the old places cannot know you any more after the flesh, in spirit you may be always fit to fill them.

Do you know that really your Covenant day decided for you the answer to the question I want to ask on the strength of yours to me? What did you mean when you covenanted: 'I give myself to God, and here and now bind myself to Him in a solemn covenant: I will love and trust and serve Him supremely so long as I live'? Did it not mean that you were ready to accept God's will in whatever He allowed? Did you not then finally renounce the right to choose the pleasant and congenial way? Did it not mean saying in some way to God from your heart:

> Me if Thy grace vouchsafe to use,
>   Meanest of all Thy creatures me,
>   The deed, the time, the manner choose.

What led you to such a pledge?

1. The revelation that had come to your own heart clearly and unmistakably, showing you that God asked it of you.

2. The answering agreement of your own mind, even when you shrank from it, that such a consecration was your reasonable service.

3. The world's need of people in whose lives self had ceased to hold the right to demand attention.

What has changed you, dear J____? Is it merely that the devil presents the temptation in a new way? I beg of you, consider carefully before you decide to leave by your own request the place in which God has permitted you to be placed. God does not change. He calls us still to perfect obedience and trust. *You* must not change. Stand by your covenant and it shall be God's responsibility to bring you through. He will not fail; and even in this experience you shall prove how true it is that 'Nothing is by chance in our lives; if we trust Him, all is by love.' Yes, even this uncongenial spot, its difficult and disappointing ground, the questioning uncertainty of the future; all is by love, that you, the loved one, might be perfected; perfected as He, the Firstborn, was perfected, through suffering, through loss, through temptation.

When X___ has done for you all God intends it should, He will know how to remove you; but do you have patience to wait His time, else you will miss some finishing or purifying touch that cannot come to you in any other place than that in which you now are. You are God's, and while you are wholly given up to His will, 'I am persuaded that neither death, nor life, nor angels, nor principalities, nor powers (nor DCs), nor things present, nor things to come . . . shall be able to separate you from the love of God.' His love makes the place He chooses for you the best place. Do not take yourself out of love's way; but trust the wisdom and the power of the Father to change the course of the stars before He allows a sanctified soul to be in the wrong place.

I am still holding to this, which was what I believed when I signed my covenant. I mean to believe it to the end. How interesting it will be then to look back and see why God allowed the things that seemed so strangely wrong.

I count on you to fulfil your covenant. It was made in all sincerity. Keep it in all truth.

Yours, bound by the same pledges

PS—Do be good to the new girls. You know how trembly you felt inside, whether you showed it or not, during those first weeks on the field. Give them a kind word, and do help them in every way you can to be as good as they ought.

5

THE MANAGEMENT OF ONE'S DAYS

JUNE 1914

My Dear H____,

It seems to me you expect a sort of encyclopaedia by way of a letter! Perhaps if you had made more use of the question box when you were here you might have gone forth better equipped with information. Still, you know it always pleases me when folk ask questions, and I shall just do the best I can in the way of answers.

I think I told you once, or perhaps more than once, when you were here, that if your heart were in your work as an Army officer, you would always have more to do than you could do; and I quite agree with you that to have a plan does help you to do the very most, which is what we are aiming at all the time. On the other hand, I found that hard-and-fast rules as to the day's or week's work are not practicable in an FO's life. So many things that go to make up an average week are not the things we reckon for, and often the unexpected opportunity is far more urgent and important than the duty for which we had planned.

Therefore I should advise you to have a general idea as to the sharing up of your time, but not to attempt to tie yourself to details. Even a general idea has to be modified according to the special circumstances of the locality. Hours of visitation, for instance: these should be regulated by the hours of work in the neighbourhood. In some parts you can put in the most productive visiting of the whole day after tea, making it often worth while for one of you to miss the open-air in order to visit. This time is particularly valuable for following up special cases.

In our first corps I found this a good working basis for a week. To begin with the question of the housework: this can be made good fun and a real relaxation if you both take an interest in it. My lieutenant was best at the house, and I at the cooking; so she did upstairs and laid breakfast, while I did downstairs, got the breakfast, and started preparing dinner.

After breakfast we finished dinner preparations (it was often partly cooked while we had breakfast), and, with the help of a gas stove, we could leave puddings, soups, pies, etc., to cook in the oven while we were out. The fact that the food was prepared and cooking always provided us with a common-sense reason for declining when we were asked to stay out to dinner. In this way we had a properly-cooked meal every day without robbing ourselves of too much time. The half hour for prayer was fitted in for one of us after breakfast and for one after dinner, while the other washed up, etc. These plans applied to every morning.

Monday morning, the lieutenant did the washing, and I did all the business outstanding. If I finished in time I helped with the washing, but always cooked the dinner. Afternoon and sometimes part evening, visiting of converts. Of course, there were times when we were off first thing on Monday morning to follow up a special case. Tuesday, Wednesday, and Thursday we reckoned to be out visiting by between 9.30 and 10 a.m. In for about an hour and a quarter to dinner. Afternoon and evening, visiting—according to the time of the meeting. Friday morning was spent by us both in prayer and preparation for the week-end meetings; then an early dinner, followed by a long afternoon's visitation. Saturday morning, cleaning and mending; afternoon, visiting; and, of course, always booming the pubs at night.

Occasionally we spent a free evening each; and if I were starting in the field now I should take this regularly for health of body, mind, and soul. If you have no evening free from meetings, plan it so that one can carry through the work while the other rests. You can always leave something in the way of supper handy, and the on-duty one can come in without disturbing the off-duty one. I think you will find this workable with variations.

As to your business—I should dearly love to come and do an inspection, and congratulate you on having fixed up a desk. My first one was made out of an old washstand, but it did excellent service. I do hope you are really improving. I do not consider you are naturally good at business, but that is no reason why you should not drill yourself so as to be able to say with justice: 'Where I was weak there I am strong.'

Promptness and accuracy does mean a saving of time for you and for others, to say nothing of other things. Get a few good strong clips, so that you can always have your papers sorted and in order. Never toss them down anywhere, but clip them up immediately with the bundle to which they belong. Keep all matters still requiring attention in a prominent place, making it a rule to go through every paper each Monday; filing away or destroying those that are finished with, and dealing with everything as far as possible up to date.

You will find it best for yourself, and helpful for the lieutenant, that she should take some definite responsibility. For instance, the question of the publications. Help her to get into it, and then hold her entirely responsible for having the books properly entered up, for obtaining money or returns from all boomers, and having everything ready for you to despatch on Monday; going yourself through the items, returns, money owing, and cash.

This is more important, perhaps, than it seems. Unbusinesslike methods here have led some of our young people into temptation. We ought to work so that it shall be as difficult as possible for people to do wrong in anything in which they are connected with us.

Slackness in this respect makes it so easy, especially for those whose standards are not high, to think lightly of what really amounts to appropriating to their own use what is not theirs. It may take a little time and trouble to get this on to a proper footing; but when once it is done you will not only save time and trouble, but you will find that your people will take a pride in working the thing on the right lines.

I am ever so glad you and ____ get on well together. I hoped you would. Be sure you watch for each other in all that has to do with your spiritual welfare. You have such an opportunity to influence one another, perhaps very much more than you realize. Pray together about the corps and the people. Oneness in prayer makes for oneness in other things.

How fortunate that you have a second bedroom! Because however jolly you are together, I do feel that a little corner of your own is essential. If it is only an attic, and a mattress on the floor, to *yourself*, you are better off than if you shared the best furnished room with someone else. It may be bare enough, but to you it can be a sanctuary—a holy spot, where you meet God alone, and talk to Him face to face. Besides which, it is a sort of harbour into which you can sail for a few minutes' peace in the time of storm; and where, too, you can have a fit of the blues on your own without running the risk of infecting your comrade—for the blues are catching! There are times for every soul when to be alone is a necessity. It is one of my worries here that so few of the girls get a 'cube' of their own; but we must keep believing for perfection in the shape of a new training college one day.

With regard to the visiting, I should say emphatically, *go together*, if at all possible, especially when you visit soldiers. For sick, and house-to-house visitation, this is not so important. Under this heading, I cannot resist reminding you of FO classes, and the oft-repeated advice which was wiser than you guessed: 'Do not go out to meals.'

We could send you the mustard from here, but you ought to be able to get it from any reliable chemist. Ask for mustard bran. You cannot do better than put your feet in mustard and water for colds and headaches, and it is not much trouble. Set up a hydro of your own, and practise on each other.

I do not know whether I have gone as nearly round the world as you intended me to, but I must find time to tell you that it pleases me to know you are still saved above side combs! One of the girls wrote the other day, that she found her side combs at the bottom of her box, and decided that she should like to wear them; but putting them on seemed to raise the question: 'Is this a step back?' A few minutes' thought and prayer ended in the smashing of the combs.

I hope my attempts to take the place of the encyclopaedia will encourage you to ask as many more questions as you want. It is, perhaps, the greatest pleasure of all to feel that I can be of some little help to you old girls.

May the Lord be with you continually, bringing to perfection His purposes for you. I think I have already sent you this little verse of Bonar's; but I send it again. It is a prayer I pray for myself as well as for you:

> Less, less of self each day,
>   And more, my God, of Thee;
> Oh, keep me in the way,
>   However rough it be.
> Leave naught that is unmeet
>   Of all that is mine own;
> Grip me, and so complete
>   My training for the Throne.

Yours, to serve you

6
DOWN AMONGST THE CRANKY, CREEPY, CROOKED FOLK

My Dear D____,

You sound rather fagged! I am sorry, for I know how different men and things are likely to appear as a result. I wish I could land you here by some sort of magic, and give you one or two days away from everything that belongs to X____ corps. I would rest you, feed you, and chat things over with you; and, after a meeting or two in which you could give the sergeants a bit of your field experience, as well as get a cheer up in your own soul, send you back. I wish I could, but I can't.

However, before I start on the more serious subject of my letter, I am going to push in a bit of advice in the hope that it may come to you at a moment when you are sensible enough to take it. I know you, and the way you 'keep at it'. I would not change you in that respect for worlds; but I quite mean it when I say: decide to leave your work alone for a whole twenty-four hours. Arrange with lieutenant, if you feel you cannot both be off at the same time, that she shall do the meeting and all necessary business. Start by sleeping on as long as you can in the morning; then do mending or writing, just as you feel inclined. Eat as little dinner as possible; read a little while after, and then go for a walk—not a visit.

I wish you were in the country, for if you hate walking in streets as much as I do, you won't enjoy it; but all the same, go. Take a 'bus ride, and walk back, at any rate. Walk until you are well tired, then come in to tea—not more than two cups! Eat sparingly again. After tea have a little time alone to read and pray without being in a hurry. Pray about your people, and tell the Lord how you feel. Then about 7 p.m. start getting ready for bed. Finish up by putting your feet into hot water and drinking a glass of warm milk. Be settled down and have your light out by 8 o'clock. Never mind if you do not feel sleepy. Rest, in the dark, is the next best thing to sleep for the body; besides, you might go to sleep after all.

If you would do this when you feel like you did when you wrote me, I am sure you would find it helpful. Do not laugh at the idea—try it! I know you are too busy, but you will get through more in the end. Let lieutenant take over everything, as though you were not there. You cannot see things in their true relationship when you are nervy and done, and it rather plays into the devil's hands to drag on. A few hours' extra sleep, and a little less to eat, would save many a defeat and put to flight many a doubt. A day in time saves—who can tell how many? So much for that.

I only wish you could have time to carry out this advice before you read the next portion of my letter. If you had, what I say would probably seem more reasonable. Your people, you say, are so unsatisfactory, so cold, so far from all they ought to be, that you feel that after P____ you simply cannot stand it. You have tried honestly, you say. I know what that means—you have been doing a month's work in a week's time, but you see little difference! At P____ the people responded; they were in a good spirit; their zeal and love helped you. Now, if you help one, you offend another; everybody is cranky, or creepy, or crooked; and, as you say, you feel you cannot stand it.

Now I know where you are in theory, but what is the use of a theory that you do not live up to? After all, what claim have the people on you? What is it about them that draws you to them? Why did you ever think of going to any people anywhere? The same needs that attracted Jesus? If so, the more ignorant, the more halting, the more weak, the more sinful they are, the *more*, surely, will you know that you are sent to *them*—to them, the *sinners* (they may be soldiers as well), not to the righteous. The soldiers at P____ were all righteous! You are sent to the lost, not the found; to the weak, not the strong; sent to gather them into the Kingdom—the lame, the halt, and the blind of X____.

Dear D____, you are indeed sent to these people with their gossipings, deceptions, superstitions, and backslidings. Their sins call for your holiness; their weakness for your strength; their unbelief for your faith; their coldness of heart for your love and zeal. All these claim you. The people's need cries out in unmistakable accents. I know your heart cries out, too: 'Who is sufficient for these things?'

The answer is in one name—JESUS. Has He not travelled this way before you? How did His people receive Him? What about the twelve on the roll? Did not they misunderstand and fail Him? rebuke Him? doubt Him? neglect Him? run away from Him? betray Him? Yet nothing is more apparent than that He did not judge them according to the appearance, or according to their deserts, but made allowance for circumstances and temperament.

In the face of their narrowness and selfishness, their

weakness and unbelief, He never lost sight of the great fact of His life—that He came to save sinners. 'They that are whole', He said, 'have no need of a physician, but they that are sick. I came not to call the righteous, but sinners.' He went to the sinner, because He had a vision of the sinner *saved*. He went to the weary, because He had seen the possibility of the weary at *rest*; to the unclean, for he saw him '*clean* every whit'. In all, He worked and toiled, not because of what there *was*, but because of what there *might* be. The Kingdom was the grain of mustard seed: now the smallest of herbs, but presently the greatest. Peter, now the hasty, awkward, domineering runaway: presently, Peter the courageous, earnest, faithful shepherd of souls.

Your folk are just Peters and Thomases. Humanly, there is little about them to inspire even interest or hope. Below the average, you say; cranky, creepy, crooked! The whole question is whether you see *that* only, or whether there is enough of the Divine in *you* to show you the possibilities in *them*. Are you sent to the whole or to the sick; to the crooked or to the straight; to the bound or to the free?

All depends on the measure of the Divine Presence in you. If you lack there, the people's sins and failures will only call forth from you a judgment or an excuse. God does not send you to give either.

Human nature, left to itself, soon tires of helping human nature; and after arriving at the stage when you find only condemnation for the people, it is easy enough to drift to the point when you cease to hope for them. Leave out the question of what you feel. Do not stay to consider what results you see, but work the works of Him that sent you while it is day, for the time cometh when your day at X____ will end.

You are where you are because you are needed there. You must never forsake your post nor lower your standard. I realize the temptation to do the latter, which comes to all of us who live continually with those whose standards are low. But I must save that up for my next sermon!

Do take the advice I gave you at the beginning of this letter. Think things over, and finish up by singing No. 612, especially that third verse:

> Ten thousand snares my path beset;
> Yet will I, Lord, the work complete
>   Which Thou to me hast given;
> Regardless of the pains I feel,
> Close by the gates of Death and Hell,
>   I press along to Heaven.

> Yours, believing for you
> as well as for Cranky and Co.

7

SECURING FRESH PEOPLE

AUGUST 1914

My Dear B_____,

I have found time to read your long newsy letter through twice, and now that I settle down to answer it I do pray that I may be able to give you advice that will prove of some help.

First, I should like to tell you what encourages me most of all in what you say. It is this sentence: 'I have prayed and wept over them when I have been alone with God.' While you are doing this, I know it means victory in the end, whatever the difficulties and disappointments are at the moment; victory for you in your own experience; and victory, at least in some measure, amongst your people.

There is a sense in which I would rather hear of your weeping in secret over the sins of the people than I would hear of your brilliant success, accompanied by the knowledge that you had ceased to pray such prayers and to shed such tears.

I have been carefully thinking over the condition of your corps, so far as I know it. It seems to me that your greatest need at the moment is the getting hold of new people.

Probably the reason that there have been no souls saved is that your congregation is made up of saints and of really hardened God-rejectors; yet you are surrounded by a population of just the kind of people to whom we are sent. The problem is how to reach them. They do not come to your meetings, they do not listen to the open-air, and except for the little bit of outside visitation that you can find time to do, they are unreached by the Army. Yet if only you could find them, there must be a number in need of cheer and comfort, and just the sort of help that the Salvation of God and the comradely atmosphere of Salvation Armyism could give.

I am more and more impressed, from many things that I hear and see, with the terrible loneliness and hardship of the lives of crowds of people, in many cases on the very doorstep of our corps; and there ought to be some means discovered of finding them out and making them feel that some one in the world cares.

Now, I know you are working as hard as ever you can, doing as much as is possible yourself in the way of visiting. By the by, you do not tell me whether that sick man you were nursing got better. I hope he did, or else your credit as a nurse might go down; and there is a great deal in having a good name! I believe that without adding too much to your personal responsibilities, it would be possible to plan so that a number of fresh people could be reached and influenced.

Select three or four women from amongst your soldiers, not necessarily married, who would be willing to devote at least one afternoon a week to the work. These need not be people who are much on the platform; and might probably be chosen from amongst soldiers who, up to the present, have not done a great deal as fighters, but who at the same time are godly and kind-hearted. According to the number of workers available, select districts as is done for the cadets during training. These, of course, should be chosen in the poorest neighbourhoods, and should not comprise more ground than the comrades can reasonably cover.

Prepare a little book in which a record of their work can be kept, giving a space for the names and addresses of special cases, and a brief summary of weekly work, showing time spent in visitation or the number of visits made. The name of the street or streets should be entered in the book, as well as that of the comrade to whom it belongs.

Have a supply of old literature to give away, especially 'The Young Soldier'. You can get these gratis. After having advanced so far with your arrangements, fix a convenient evening when the sisters in question can be invited to tea at the quarters or elsewhere, and make this the occasion of thoroughly explaining to them the object of their work. Impress upon them their responsibility for the people in the districts thus appointed to them. They should visit them all, giving special attention whenever they find sickness, sorrow, or any particular need; invite the people to the meetings; distribute literature, and, if possible, make customers for the papers. These visitors should make a real effort to get children who do not attend a Sunday-school to come to the 'juniors'.

A cottage meeting, monthly or fortnightly, might be worked up in some districts with great advantage. Explain that, to introduce them and give them a start, you will go with each the first time they go; and that afterwards you will spend one afternoon a week with them in turn. Finish up by a little spiritual talk, and get them to pray for their people and themselves.

I believe you would find much good result from such a plan, and many extra things could be worked in as the people came to know their districts. For instance, how much cheer could be brought to the bedridden and chronically invalided people, who never can go to a place of worship, if occasionally a small group of corps cadets or converts or juniors came to sing to them.

Such little gatherings could be arranged by any of these comrades in her district, without in any sense interfering with the ordinary meetings of the corps; and, surely, anything and everything that brings our own people into more direct touch with the suffering and needs of their neighbours, must mean an enlarging of their own sympathies, and so be indirectly the means of blessing to themselves, as well as to those they try to cheer.

You could, probably, with a little arrangement, fix an open-air periodically in each of the streets thus allocated, being careful to let the visiting comrade know of it beforehand, so that she might advertise the visit and make something special of it, and make an effort herself to be present at that open-air. While it was in progress, you could slip round with her to speak to as many families as possible.

I firmly believe that you would find some definite results after carrying this out for a few weeks. Religion has not lost its power to interest the people, nor have the needs and sorrows of others ceased to appeal to the hearts of those who do love God; but the devil succeeds too well in keeping the sinner and the saint apart.

In these days the people, because they are accustomed to our marches and open-airs, are not attracted to the meetings in such crowds as they used to be; so we must seek out other means of reaching them, or we shall not get so large a proportion saved.

These visitors should act as scouts to you, bringing to your notice cases of great need or sorrow; so that literally, as far as those districts are concerned, the Army officers will be made aware without delay of any circumstances in which either practically or spiritually the people could be helped.

You should arrange to have a word with each of these comrades weekly about their people and their districts, and meet them for prayer and discussion of plans and methods once a month, on which occasion the books should be looked at and initialled by you.

Now, will you try this? It would cost you very little financially, and not take very much time; and I believe if you set the comrades to work before the winter—and especially if they were able to give a little practical help in the way of food for the sick, advice, and so on—an impression would be made on the town, as a whole, that the Army was in touch with the people. This might make it possible for you to raise funds through the local press for special relief, if that were necessary, later on. Of course, the comrades should visit in uniform always, and should be encouraged to pray, read, or sing with the people wherever possible.

Not so very long ago I heard of a corps where this sort of work, in a more limited way, was undertaken by a brigade of corps cadets on their free afternoons. Where they found sick people, and could not give the time required for extra visitation themselves, they arranged with soldiers in the corps who were willing to do so. The effect on the corps was amazing, the most encouraging results being the awakening of real interest in a number of soldiers who had been doing practically nothing, and the addition of a number of fresh people to the regular congregation.

The advantage of this idea is that it enables you to use comrades who would not be experienced enough to deal with soldiers and recruits. I know the difficulty of finding such people makes it impossible in many corps to work the ward system; but this visitation would not include the visitation of soldiers or recruits, nor interfere in any way with the existing arrangements for visitation by recruiting or visiting sergeants.

If only our days were twice as long, how easily they could be filled! But the next best thing to doing more yourself is to get others to help you. In some cases, it is better than next best, because if you can only get them practically interested and this visitation organized, the work will continue when you are gone; whereas anything you have in your own hands will suffer, even if it does not entirely come to an end, by your removal. Try it.

Nothing is worse than going on without results except giving up altogether; but I know you will not do that! To try a new plan and fail is better, I think, than to make no effort.

I wish I could come and help you. Sometimes I have an indescribable longing to be amongst the people. No other work seems to me to come so truly into harmony with the Lord's life as that in which we are in contact with sinners. Rejoice in your chance. Such are the strange contradictions of spiritual life, that tears have a place in our highest happiness; and we find ourselves 'as sorrowful, yet always rejoicing'.

By the time this reaches you we shall be in full swing with the new session. Do pray for us and for the cadets. When was there ever a greater opportunity for doing soul-saving work, if only those who attempt it are baptized by the Holy Ghost, sanctified by His Presence, and set on fire with His love? The girls will be praying for you at 'the ten minutes'. You, who know something of what is before them, bring them to God, for only He can fit them; and I believe you will get a double blessing.

May God guide you and give you your heart's desire in the Salvation of the people. I *do* believe it shall be.

Yours, full of faith for you

8
TO ONE WHO QUESTIONS GOD'S DEALINGS

SEPTEMBER 1914

My Dear G____,

How near your letter brings you! how vividly it recalls what is so easily forgotten! how clearly it tells me that, though we are separated in a hundred ways by material differences, yet our spirits tread the same road, our feet grow weary on the same stretches, and we stumble over the same places! What a travesty that the last drop in the already over-flowing cup of bitterness, the darkest hour of the darkest night, the crowning pain of the fiercest temptation, is the feeling that we *suffer alone*. The terror of spiritual darkness is that sense of isolation which envelops the soul like the chill autumn mist, shutting out every vision that could bring human comfort or consolation.

Surely, this sense of aloneness, present in greater or lesser measure with us all, is not without its meaning. Surely, every pain that a human soul is capable of suffering is but a gateway through which it may pass to a fuller joy.

Looking back at my own experience, I see how, because my unbelieving heart found it always easier to turn to the human than to the Divine, God led me by a way in which I *thought* no other soul had travelled; and when I *felt* myself alone, when in the darkness there seemed no light, when in my sorrow no sympathy from an understanding heart was within reach, *then* I cried to God: not the cry of words only, nor of mind only, nor of determination only, but the cry of my whole being, 'Save me, I perish!'

You have passed through such an experience, and know what I mean—when you have been nearly engulfed by some temptation, nearly swamped by some doubt, nearly carried away by some wave of sudden sorrow. In that moment of aloneness I learned how much I needed *God*, and in such moments I have *found* God.

Shall you pray that such experiences come no more? Shall you, because of what you suffer, only shrink from them? Dear child, no! The great need of your heart, as of the hearts of all men in all ages, is to know God; and you

35

must be brave enough to face anything that can bring you to a fuller knowledge of Him.

Remind yourself of what you have gained by such experiences in the past; and that, far from proving you are different from others in what you suffer, it is rather in itself another proof that 'there hath no temptation taken you but such as is common to man.' The form of it may be different, but what you feel in it is the same; and for you, as for others, 'the sufferings of this present time are not worthy to be compared with the glory which shall be revealed in us.' I long to help you. I know so well the depths of heart-anguish which must needs come, and that in spite of all I can say you will still feel I do not fully understand; but, oh, I pray that this very feeling may lead you to discover how fully God understands the heart He has created; and that with certainty you may say, 'But He knoweth the way that I take: when He hath tried me, I shall come forth as gold.'

My dear G____, the devil is evidently attacking you; but hold on, and God will make your very temptations a means of grace; for so He defeats the enemy.

The perpetual tendency to question God's dealings is but part of the same attack; and while you allow yourself to ask *why* He should try you as He does; *why* you should be called to pass alone through such a furnace, you are led into the temptation to question His dealings with the world.

How cunningly the devil lays his trap! He well knows the moment when a question on your part has more power to hinder than anything else. When suffering fails to daunt your courage; when temptation to sin only drives you to your knees; when the scoff of the world only fires your faith, then he comes, clothed in a mist so that you do not easily recognize him. Before you realize it, he has spread his confusing question; and, listening, you find yourself in the fog of doubt.

The only way out of that fog is to cease chasing the unsolved problems that surround you. Do not for a moment imagine that any doubting inquiry of yours can reveal or explain what God has chosen to veil and withhold.

If the problems that perplex you were all explained tomorrow, would there be any vital change in your life? Things being as they are, the explanation of mysteries would not do away with today's duties. Why not, then, do the duties that are within your reach with all faithfulness, leaving revelations and explanations to be made in God's own time: lest in seeking after what is beyond your reach you lose that which is in your hands?

Dare to renounce the temptation to analyse the actions of God. Cease to grope after the understanding of 'all mysteries', the possession of 'all knowledge'; for even if you had these, without a heart of love they would profit you nothing: whereas if you seek after love you shall find 'a more excellent way . . . for love never faileth.'

Turn from the mysteries of the universe to the mystery of your own heart. Remember with what wisdom and how perfectly God has made you to know all that is necessary to your Salvation, and be content to leave some things to be discovered in Heaven. Turn from the problems of death and Hell to the everyday problems of life and duty. Turn from the questioning of other people's holiness to the living out of your own.

I say this to you in all earnestness. There is, and ever will be, much which we cannot understand, but God has not left us in the dark about His will for ourselves. Let us be careful to walk in the light we have, lest it become darkness.

Never mind how much, at its beginnings, the way of doubt may appear a seeking after light: its end is gross darkness. Hold fast as death to the things you *do* know; and quietly spread before God, and leave with Him, the questions that arise in your heart to which you find no answer.

For your heart, as for mine, the question is not, do I *understand* God, but do I *trust* Him? Not do I *agree* with God, but do I *obey* Him? Not do I *see* God, but do I *love* Him? If we can answer to these questions 'I do', then we shall not be ashamed before Him when we see Him 'face to face'.

Yours, to help you

9

FOR LOVE OR FOR MONEY?

OCTOBER 1914

My Dear K____,

Did you ever sing it—'Stick to the Army, lasses; never run away'? It was good advice. The longer my experience grows the more truly do I feel that the Army *is* worth sticking to. It is a big thing and a joyful thing to have a share in it, and to be a part of it. I know you agree with me up to a certain point in this; but there is a place where we differ.

You say that if your health gave way—throat, or anything like that—and you found yourself physically unfit for the strain of the field, you would then feel quite justified in seeking some suitable employment outside the Army. In fact, you say you would rather do that than take up some particular branch of work for which you feel no aptitude nor any special call.

I look at it in this way. If God called you to the Army (and He certainly did), He called you to it as a whole; that your life might be devoted to its interests, and to the building up of His Kingdom within its ranks. Surely, your faith in that call should not waver, nor your obedience to it fail, because it seems likely that your work in it may be of a different character from that which you anticipated? Does not the real joy of the fully consecrated soul begin at the point when we can say, 'Lord, I am in Thy hands, up to the measure of my strength, for *any* work, at *any* time, in *any* place'?

I know you say that some work has no directly spiritual bearing, and that you might as well do such outside the Army (perhaps for a better salary) as inside the Army. But does not this wholly depend on the distinction between the two that *you* make? If to you, work done merely for gain can ever be on the same level as work done for love, then it simply means you have never raised your work to the right standard.

When I gave myself to God I gave all I was; and since that time what I do, I do unto Him. I do not consider I work for payment. Whatever I may receive in the way of money is God's, to be used in the wisest way, whether for my own needs or for the needs of others. I reckon the work I do ought always to be worth more to the Army than anything I get; else, where will my giving come in?

Further, when I gave myself to God I decided He would know how to overrule so that I might be placed where He willed. I made no reserves; and while some kinds of work would not be so congenial to me as others, I can truly say that that willingness for anything is still a part of my consecration; and I know well that the moment I departed from it the devil would begin to torture me with the prospect of going just where I was not prepared to go.

It is not then, you see, a question in my mind whether you could or could not do the same thing 'outside' as 'in', but a question of *the motive for which you work*. If the motive be right, it should hold good without variation, whether your work happens at the moment to be preaching or nursing, teaching a neglected child to run a seam, or typing a page of manuscript, peddling, or collecting, or any other 'ing'. The character of the work is the least important. The spirit in which you do it is what decides whether it will be acceptable to God and profitable to yourself and other souls.

To me, the difference between working at anything *for the sake of the wage*, and working *as an offering to God*, is all the difference between life and death, between things temporal and things eternal.

I want you to think about it wisely. Do not wait until you are actually faced with the necessity to choose— then it may be too late. You will probably be harassed with many anxious thoughts, and it will be impossible to face the prospect of a change in an impartial state of mind. Some girls for whom I had hoped great things made just such a mistake. One, who would not consider 'institution life' in the Army for the Lord's sake, with an opportunity of helping the inmates of the institution in their souls, has landed in an institution for imbeciles, where no attempt on spiritual lines is allowed, even if it could avail. Another, who had it in her to do something worthy, is full up with clerical and financial work at a good salary, spending life for no higher end than the securing of her own bread and butter, and this after having once consecrated herself for the service of the King.

I think the life of a lieutenant in the slums, or even a scrubber in the shelter, doing her little bit out of love to God, is nearer the mark of the high calling in Christ Jesus.

I do not believe either of those girls would have left if their consecration had been fully made at a time when they were free from the pressure of sickness or special temptation. If it had been, then when the trial came, there would have been no way in for the devil and his plausible arguments.

To turn aside meant drawing back from their consecration; and this, I am sure, they did not mean to do. The mistake was, that they had never settled the question; never really decided their willingness to do *any*thing; and because in the moment of difficulty they found themselves only willing to do *some* things, the devil knew how to make it look as though they could do nothing!

You may be faced with the necessity of a change for your work's sake as much as for your own. Can you say, 'The deed, the time, the manner choose'? If you write and tell me that you can, I shall be at rest about you, for I know God will control for you, and all will be well. *But reservations have power to spoil all*. You will remember the old Training College story about the cadet who sang 'Anywhere but Scotland', and, of course, was commissioned there—and had a very good time, too!

Well, don't you have a 'but' in *your* consecration. Be ready to pitch in and do your very best wherever God allows your leaders to send you, or in whatever branch of work a place for you can be found. Your anxiety about the future will be less from the very moment that you settle this.

Only two qualities in you are wanted to bring you to the point where I long to see you: faith in God, and love for the Army. You need the faith that sings, even when you suffer:

> I will trust Thee,
> All my life Thou shalt control.

You need the love that says in all sincerity, 'I had rather be a doorkeeper in the Salvation Army than dwell in the tents of the outsiders.'

K____, without the believing and the loving, how impossible all real Salvation Army work is! But if we believe and love truly all things *are* possible.

As for me, the joy, the wonder, the heaven of being able to dedicate my bit of life, actually in everyday sayings and doings to the service of God, grows continually more real. Not that it costs less, not that temptations and trials and tears are fewer; but the truth is, I love it more and more; and when you serve because you love, lots of things do not count.

I have a quaint old book of translated hymns and this is one of my many favourites:

> How blessèd from the bonds of sin
> And earthly fetters free,
> In singleness of heart and aim,
> Thy servant, Lord, to be!

The hardest toil to undertake
  With joy at Thy command,
The meanest office to receive
  With meekness at Thy hand.

With willing heart and longing eyes,
  To watch before Thy gate,
Ready to run the weary race,
  To bear the heavy weight.

Thus may I serve Thee, gracious Lord!
  Thus ever Thine alone;
My soul and body given to Thee,
  The purchase Thou hast won.

Through evil or through good report,
  Still keeping by Thy side;
And by my life or by my death,
  Let Christ be magnified!

Yours, under the dear flag

10

NOW IS THE ACCEPTED TIME

NOVEMBER 1914

My Dear M____,

It is a long time since I had a line from you. I wonder how things are with you, and whether these days of great opportunity find you alive to their importance.

At the beginning of this session, in fact during the rush that preceded the arrival of the cadets, I scrawled with the office blue pencil on an envelope one morning the words, '*Now is the accepted time.*' I stuck a spike through it, and stood it up amongst my pens and pencils, where, according to the words of Joshua, it 'remaineth unto this day'.

Putting those words where I could always see them was the result of something that had happened before that morning. Most things happen as a result of something else. Perhaps if we could always realize this, we should be more careful. There are laws of continuity in the spiritual world, and one step arises out of another.

But to come to what led to sticking up those words amongst my pens. I was praying one evening, getting ready for morning 'Guide' around the breakfast table with the sergeants who, in those days, were pretty busy cleaning, making beds, etc., and, as is often the case, I found the Lord impressing on my own heart first the lesson I was to try and impress on them.

It came to me from those familiar words, 'Now is the accepted time: behold, now is the day.' It was not altogether a new lesson, yet I understood its meaning in a new way.

One of my miseries has always been that the enemy of souls knows so well how to take advantage of my valleys and hills! Something after this is his style. When I am on the hill, and it is a glorious sensation to face the world, the day and its duties, with the feeling that you're glad you're alive, to be impatient of the few minutes you spend over breakfast because you are so keen to be 'on the job'; well, I say, when I am on the hill, *I look forward*, one can see so far ahead from the hill-top, and I find my mind filled with wondrous plans. I begin calculating with exceeding joy how much I shall get through during the coming weeks. Then I am led on until presently I am planning what shall be done *next* session, how much better I shall organize this, how I shall guard against that, an extra meeting in here, half an hour's extra reading there, I shall study this, and accomplish the other.

The more I think of it, the more possible it all seems, and I go on in the happy hope sometimes many days. I go to sleep thinking, and wake up with that vague yet comfortable sensation that something good is going to happen. Then sooner or later I come down from the hilltop, sometimes suddenly, sometimes slowly; but sooner or later, I come down!

I shall not bother you with details of the kind of things that bring me down—probably they are not the same as in your case.

Then the valley! Oh, how often the enemy meets me in the valley, and the darkness grows darker, and the depths to which my spirit sinks get deeper! *I look back then.* There seems to be a fascination about it. I notice that nearly always when I can see nothing ahead, if I look back I can see ever so clearly heaps of things I had either forgotten or else not noticed much when I was actually in them.

I look back, and I see all that ought to be there and is not. Horrid condemning ghosts of the things I could have done, and did not do! I see what I might probably have accomplished if I had only persevered in spite of being tired. I see what would have happened if only I had taken some particular opportunity of dealing with a soul. There seems to be a whole host of ghosts at times, and they might have been real accomplished facts if . . . But they are ghosts, and they haunt the valley until it becomes unendurable.

I see, too, all sorts of incomplete things. Things I began and never finished; broken resolutions; hideous halves and quarters; until I begin to feel so ashamed of the past, that I am not surprised by the suggestion that, if this is what has been, it is certainly no use hoping that at my time of life I shall ever do any better.

Sometimes I remain in the valley a long time. Perhaps it is a long valley; or it may merely be that I am slow in getting through.

This is a fanciful way of expressing what I mean, but do you understand? Are we not all in danger from this kind of attack? The future is not ours. We look ahead, we fill our days with resolves, we are always intending to do better and be better—tomorrow, next week, next year, next corps; instead of saying *now*. We build hopefully on the changes that we imagine will make it easier to work wonders for God; whereas in actual fact, wonders always represent work, and the only change needed to bring them about is a change in the faith and zeal of the worker.

Some things would be easier to tackle, you thought, after you left the Training College. You shelved them while you were here. Have you launched out yet, or are you still looking ahead to some time when you will do so? Perhaps you are in the valley just now, looking back under the influence of physical weariness or some momentary disappointment. Does it seem as though the past only multiplies regrets?

Oh, how perseveringly the devil tries to blind us to the possibilities of the present, by the very tears we shed over the past! Is what *has been* to be everlastingly a measure of what *is to be*?

Besides, the past is not always so bad as it seems, when we see it from the valley. There are many things accomplished to the glory of God—many Ebenezers, but we do not review them often enough. Real things are often hidden by the dark in the spiritual as well as in the physical world, and the unreal assume an altogether convincing aspect, whereas it only needs a ray of light to dispel them.

The devil's purpose is to rob us of *now*. I have seen the danger before, but that day when I was praying for a message for my girls, I saw more clearly than ever how the principle, the message of that familiar verse can be applied all the way.

Now is the day of Salvation, now is the *accepted* time—the time for faith, the time for daring, the time for new things in my experience and in my work. If I see where an improvement could be made, 'Now is the accepted time.' So I took the old words home to my heart in a new sense, and they stand where I can see them while I write. I was tempted to postpone writing this until tomorrow morning, but they reminded me that 'now is the only time I am sure of'!

I do not know if this finds you most tempted to look forward or to look backward; whether you are comforting yourself about the unsatisfactory things in the present by hoping for something better by and by; or excusing the failure of today because of the failure of yesterday. If you are inclined to do either, concentrate all your strength on today.

Now is the accepted time! The *accepted* time, the time to believe, to love, to suffer, to achieve. *Now* is mine. The past *was* mine, the future *may* be mine, but the present *is* mine.

Why not make today the richer for the lesson of yesterday? Turn the hopes that centre round tomorrow into facts that belong to today?

With God all things are—not will be, but are—

possible. Lord, I do today, now, believe it!
Now and always

Yours, to serve you

11

A CHRISTMAS LETTER

DECEMBER 1914

My Dear Girls,

I have been trying to decide to whom I shall write this month, but there are so many of you, and somehow I want to write to you all.

The fact is, Christmas is coming! The cadets are talking about recess; and I am thinking of you old girls, for whom Christmas will not mean recess, but rather a little more work than usual. So, instead of addressing my letter to one of you, I write it to greet *any* of you who have not grown too high and mighty to remember yourselves as 'my girls'.

You will all be too busy to read a long letter when this reaches you, and I am too busy to write one. I greet you! God be with you these days—the last of the old year; days when we shall all be reminded in some way of that wonderful and holy mystery, the coming of Jesus.

The other evening, reading and praying alone in my room, there came to my heart such a real consciousness that He is 'alive for evermore'. I, and perhaps some of you, need to 'consider Him' more constantly; not only believing that He *was* but realizing that He *is* 'at the right hand of God, who also maketh intercession for us.'

To me, it seems that *the more we can realize the personality of Jesus* the more definitely our love will go out to Him.

As I grow to understand this better, I feel I grasp more fully the meaning of Paul's cry, 'I count all things but loss . . . that I may know Him.' To know Him is to love Him. To know Him more is to love Him more. And more love means more doing of those things that, apart from love, would be impossible.

I cannot, I think, wish you any richer blessing through the coming year than that you should 'grow . . . in the knowledge of our Lord and Saviour Jesus Christ', and 'that your love may abound more and more'; and that, in the strength of love, you may make the new days richer in service and sacrifice than any that have gone before.

I have chosen four words that have already been a blessing to me, as a special message for the New Year. They are these: 'Yet for Love's Sake'. The world just now is ringing with the story of deeds done and sacrifices made for the sake of honour, of duty, of patriotism, of justice; and a call comes to my heart, as clearly as any of these, to be up and doing, to be serving and giving—'for love's sake'.

I pray that, should we be tempted one day to choose the easy way through a difficulty (or round it), 'yet for love's sake' we may tackle it boldly. Should we feel justified at some point in considering ourselves, instead of our work, 'yet for love's sake' we may keep the Kingdom first.

Many times in the past the devil has been, and many more times in the future shall be, defeated. He cannot measure the strength of love. The world does not calculate that what I could not do for money, or from a sense of duty, or for the sake of success, 'yet for love's sake' I *can* do.

The way is lonely sometimes, 'yet for love's sake' we must press on. Those for whom we spend ourselves do fail us, 'yet for love's sake' let us hope again. Our good is evil spoken of, 'yet for love's sake' we can forgive.

My dear girls, it is not merely a beautiful theory, is it? We have proved the truth of it in a measure, but we do not yet 'comprehend . . . what is the breadth, and length, and depth, and height' of the love of Christ. Lord, give us more! And when courage fails us, when patience is exhausted, and when even faith wavers, 'yet for love's sake' we shall hold on.

> For the touch
>   Of Love transfigures
> All the road
>   And all its rigours.
> Life and Death
>   Love's touch transfigures
> Life and Death
>   And all that lies
> In between,
>   Love sanctifies.

Well, a happy Christmas to you! Be as glad as you can, and dry as many tears as you can (other people's, of course); and when the devil says 'you can't', answer, 'yet for love's sake' I can!

Yours, serving for love

12

THE NEW CONVERT

JANUARY 1915

My Dear R____,

Following up our conversation, I am writing you a few of my thoughts on the question of our responsibility for the newly-saved.

As I said to you, I *do* feel we are in a special sense called to consider and care for those who are 'babes in Christ'. Do not the needs and struggles of your own heart teach you to yearn for those who are only beginners?

Sometimes, I think, I have made a mistake in worrying too much and not taking sufficiently into account God's own care for them; but certainly I would rather do that than find I had neglected anything that would have made the way plainer or saved some soul from looking back. It is because I feel the matter to be one of such vital importance, that I want to add to what I said to you when you came to see me the other day.

There are some things that cannot be done at any other time, which can and ought to be done for souls during the first weeks following their conversion; at least, it is so in the majority of cases; and certainly there is much that cannot be done later, except with infinite trouble. It is like the difference between forming a habit in a child, and changing the habits of a middle-aged man.

A soul can be led during the first weeks to a place which it may take years to reach, if the opportunity of those early days be neglected.

Whose fault is it that there are today amongst us so many silent soldiers, so many worldly, so many content to be doing nothing for other souls? Nearly always the blame could be laid at the door of those who were the overseers of their souls during the first weeks of their spiritual life. Wisely dealt with, most of such soldiers could have been initiated in a way of service and sacrifice, in which they would still be found.

Do not think that God can do without you in this. If He calls you to seek the lost; if, as the shepherd, you are to find the sheep, how much more are you as the shepherd to *feed* the sheep when found?

In a very real sense the human element comes in. I have known cases where a word of inquiry, a stepping out of the way to shake hands, has made the difference between life and death.

Some people, I know, may tell you that there is a danger of getting the people saved to yourself. Well, if that is the way that leads them to God, why not? If only half of them come through and get really saved in the end, is it not worthwhile?

We are 'mothers in Israel'; and when is the mother's care more tender or more actual and constant than through those months when the little frame lies in her arms helpless, unable even to recognize or express its needs? So it seems to me, your care as a 'mother in Israel' should be most watchful, most patient, most wise, while you are nursing to vigour and maturity the flickering flame of holy desire, the new life of the Spirit, against which so many dangers conspire.

Do let your part—the human part, which is within your reach—be done; and then, even if there is a failure and the new life goes out, quenched instead of burning up into a flame, you will not need to reproach yourself.

During the first weeks I do not think you can take too much notice of converts. You are wonderful in their eyes. Often you do not realize how much a look can do to make them feel welcome, or, better still, to feel *wanted*. Be up to all kinds of dodges in order to produce such a feeling. I recall now an incident of a convert who was helped just in this way because he was given charge of the Adjutant's concertina case. You do not play one? Why not learn? It would save your throat. But your tambourine (which, by the way, I hope you have not become too respectable to use), or your song book, or a bundle of 'Crys', would do just as well.

Have a word ready: a question referring to home affairs, showing that you remember; or a remark indicating your approval of any change in dress, etc. Always remember, if they have been absent, to let them know you noticed it. All this costs you nothing, but it produces much.

An actual kindness to them or to a member of their family goes a long way. Popping in on a washing day, to give the wife or mother a lift; running in with a few flowers you have begged from somewhere, to make the tea table look nice; or with a biscuit for the baby. This sort of thing will give you a place of influence from which you may dictate to them on matters of highest import, and find them willing to obey, 'It's what captain says.' They need no higher authority!

And all the time remember *God's part*. The Divine Helper and Teacher. Lead them to Him. Teach them to pray by praying with them, and by making them pray with you; and, above all, pray *for them*. Tell them that you do. Let them feel that it is a thing to count on.

I think, you will find—probably you have done

already—that to bring people to God makes them dear to you in a special sense. Every time your heart really goes out to God for them, you are joining yourself to them in a bond of Divine love and solicitude.

Act, too, as though you really think they are saved. I truly believe sometimes that folk have dropped back into unbelief because of a lack of faith in them and for them by those who were their leaders. To inspire souls with an assurance of your confidence is a great thing, and some will hold on against desperate odds rather than let you down. You appeal to the highest in man when you trust him; and from the moment you put the ribbon on his coat you should make your convert feel you count on him to be faithful and worthy.

You are beginning a new year. Why not make a careful record of all souls—men, women, and children—converted under you, or under your care; following up each case, and see how far you can make something satisfactory of every one? How we work and labour and struggle and sacrifice to get them to the penitent-form, and then . . .!

I really think the quality of your work in the after-care of souls could be improved. Why not make a special point of it this year? It seems to me, unquestionably, the most important responsibility you have.

I once heard of an officer who said, 'If after a week the convert is still turning up to the meetings, I reckon it is a good case, and look him up; but if he is not doing well, I do not bother about him!' To me, such an attitude does not savour of the Spirit of Jesus.

This is the last thing you should allow to suffer. However busy you may be—whoever may be neglected, do not fail in your care of the beginner.

I had thought of giving you a few practical suggestions, but I shall make this too long a rigmarole if I do. I will do so next time I write. But, oh, I do want you to do better in this matter. I am sure you ought, and believe you think so yourself. *Do* promise the Lord that you will.

Remember, I want you to be a *real* success, and my ideal, as far as looking after converts is concerned, is pretty high. But I am believing.

God give you the best of New Years! Let us trust Him more, and obey Him perfectly through every new day.

Yours, to serve

13
MORE ABOUT THE CARE OF CONVERTS

FEBRUARY 1915

Dear R____,

My mind still turns to the subject of my last letter, and I do not know that at the moment anything occurs to me that seems more important than this question of the converts.

I wish I knew how to help you to see that in this connexion the small things are vital. You are, or you used to be, a plucky little soul, and I should feel I could count on you to respond bravely if I were about to propound some grand new theory, to invite you to some tremendous effort, or call you to a greater sacrifice. But when it comes merely to reminding you of things you already know, and telling you again something I have told you before, well, I wonder if it *is* any good? Perhaps as I go on writing, faith and hope will creep in. Anyway, here are a few of the hints referred to in my last.

The penitent-form. Whether you have your hand on them before they kneel there or not, when once the penitents *are* there, there should be no fear of missing you. It may not always be wise or possible for you to deal with them yourself (only be careful that those who do, know how), but you should, at least, have a definite word with each, that you may be satisfied they have really obtained Salvation. Make sure that they have been urged to confess their sin and made to pray *aloud* themselves.

If only my short experience had been yours, you would understand how I feel. How often I have seen, even in the Training College, lives spoiled, as far as service and usefulness are concerned, because of the havoc wrought by sin not confessed, or by a besetment not dealt with effectively at the penitent-form.

Don't you see that in those first moments of seeking, the soul is *ready*, in its sense of need, *to speak* of things that, later, it will be almost impossible to approach? The very circumstances give the dealer with souls the right to inquire and instruct.

Oh, the anguish, the humiliation, the marring of the souls of men, because in the beginning of their relationship with God there was no hand wise, strong, and tender enough to put in the knife and deal with the deadly thing!

I say again, either do it yourself, or else make sure some one else does it; and, in either case, have your own personal word. Unless the number of seekers be great, it ought to be easily possible for you to do this, even if it means putting the prayer meeting for the time into other hands. Often the change might be acceptable and helpful.

This moment of personal contact gives you the chance of doing several important little things; at least, *I* call them important. For instance, find out what day and hour it will be most convenient to visit them—or, if they cannot be visited, their relatives. Press home what meetings you especially want them to attend. In this connexion I should always single out the converts' meeting, the soldiers' meeting, and the Sunday morning meeting; urging attendance at the very next open-air.

Then, your final touch should be the pinning on of the ribbon. Now, do not just smile, and say to yourself, 'Oh, FO class.' Why not do it? Honestly, now, why not? Perhaps if you admitted the reason, you would be ashamed of it, and mend your ways in this respect.

My dear R____, I *believe* in it. It is a strength for the weak, a joy to the strong, and often a support to the shaky. In fact, I have known it positively the means of Salvation—when some poor drunk has found it on his coat without remembering for the moment how it got there! It has been a link that has held him, bound hand and foot, till he has found his way in earnest to the Cross.

You say some folk will not live up to it. No; of course they won't. Many who profess to be Christians do not live up to it, but you would not discourage any one from professing to be a Christian for that reason, would you? Besides, remember what I said to you about making them feel *you had faith for them*. Here is your chance right away.

It is the Army mark, and separates them at once from the world, so paving the way for further teaching as to dress, etc.

Try a testimony, right there and then—good, bad, or indifferent! It cannot do harm. Of course, in some cases it is a wonderful help to take them home, or send some one with them, especially if they are under any sort of bondage to the drink.

Then the visiting. Whenever possible, go to see them somehow on the following day. The quicker you turn up the greater effect your visit is likely to have either on the convert or on his relations. Let some soldier or recruit call for them in time for the open-air, and at the first they attend get them to *do* something. They will hardly dare to disobey you then. Ask them to give out the verse of a song, or speak, or sing, or both, or all! Take no refusal. Offer to sing with them. In fact, do anything to get the ice broken that first night; and, in nine cases out of ten, it will not freeze again.

You say it is a risk. Yes; but in what field is anything won apart from risk. You never take a step without running the risk of falling! You never sip your tea without being in danger of choking! Your converts may not all stand, but, believe me, *a larger proportion of them will*, if you risk them in this way straight off. You see, it helps them to feel different, besides adding the tremendous weight of a definite public confession of Christ to their own sense of responsibility before God.

The converts' meeting. First, I say, *have it!* Have it, if you have only one convert! *What madness to expect people to KNOW what they ought to be and do when no one has taught them!* I believe the Holy Spirit works miracles in this direction, but He does not do what you are put there to do. Even a Paul needed an Ananias; how much more our Pollies and Bills, to whom often the voice of Jesus has not been as clear as it was to Paul that day on the road to Damascus.

I think three-quarters of an hour or an hour before the soldiers' meeting is the best time for the converts' meeting. You can vary it in many ways. Include the recruits, and make it a preparation class for soldiership. Go through the soldiers' regulations. Let them, of course, be supplied with their own copy, and encourage them to mark and add notes as you expound.

Give short talks on practical subjects, such as: how to pray, how to read the Bible, how to testify in the open-air, etc. Invite them to speak as to difficulties and problems; and, unless I am very much mistaken, your converts' meeting will be like the dew of Heaven to your own soul.

After all, what is the use of telling you things you already know? Better, perhaps, than writing to you, would it be to spend the time praying for you; praying that the spirit of the Shepherd may possess you—making you a shepherd who will lay down his life rather than lose any of the flock.

Such a spirit has its springs in a love for souls; and if your heart has really yearned over them, then you will want to keep them. Then there will be in your heart an echo, and on your lips a crying out, and in your hands an actual expression of the words of the chief Shepherd: 'I will search My sheep, and seek them out . . . I will feed them in a good pasture . . . I will seek that which was lost, and bring again that which was driven away, and will bind up that which was broken, and will strengthen that which was sick.'

That for such a work the Holy Spirit may strengthen your hands and inspire your heart, my dear R___, is the prayer of

Yours, to serve you

PS—I need not say to you, need I, that, of course, all the above applies in just the same way, *whether the converts are yours or your predecessor's*.

14
TO ONE SORROWING

MARCH 1915

My Dear E____,

You are just now needing help I cannot give. Although the place of sorrow is the place where souls come closer together than they do in any other, it is also just there that our sense of separation floods in like an isolating tide. How near, and yet how far we are even from those we love!

I have not many hopes about Heaven; but this is one of them: that with freedom from the flesh will come the possibility of such communion with the spirit of another as shall make us able to enter into each other's feelings, and to know the measure of the cup of sorrow or joy each drank alone. 'Now we see through a glass darkly—then face to face.'

It will be worth while having a 'personal' then! I shall know exactly what you feel and mean, and you will know exactly what I feel and mean. But we are not in Heaven yet; not even near enough on earth to sit over the fire and talk out that in our own hearts that words *could* express.

By the time this is in your hands, the first days of stunning grief will have passed, and you will be left with what is, perhaps, the most difficult of all—the taking up of the threads of each day's duty, while you face afresh every morning, and take home to your heart every evening, that sense of emptiness which seems almost to swallow up the things that remain.

I should like to be able to put my arms around you, and let the silence of sympathy comfort, if it could, when the sound of it would only jar. Such a desire is quite impracticable. Even if it could help, it could only be for a moment. And you must face life—life with that sense of emptiness in it—life with that other life gone out of it. But, my dear child, if God is to be glorified, you must face it in such a way that the shadow lies behind, and not ahead. Your spirit must not dwell in the darkness of the grave, but in the light of Heaven. You must not walk through life holding death's icy hand, but holding to a living faith that, in the very presence of death, warms your heart with a hope that has its kindlings in the everlasting love of the unchanging Father.

Sorrows must come; we know that. We are reconciled even to the thought that to follow Jesus means a multiplying rather than a lessening of our griefs. How could it be otherwise when He was a Man of Sorrows, acquainted with grief? If we who follow Him were without sorrows and losses, how should we find in ourselves a true oneness, a living sympathy with Him, and with the hearts all round us who sorrow, and who sorrow without God?

I cannot stand between you and the blow, nor do I know any way by which I can banish the burden that lies on your heart; but I long to help you to that attitude of soul which turns your sorrow into your salvation—the saving in you of so much that might easily be lost just now.

It seems to me a great grief is like a furnace—it either refines or destroys: like a mighty wind, it either tears up by the roots the faith of years, or, sweeping over it, leaves it strengthened and established. *You* must decide which it shall be. The attitude of your soul, not the storm of sorrow that sweeps over it, will determine whether you remain rooted and grounded: the spirit in your heart, not the furnace of affliction through which it passes, will determine whether you come forth as gold.

If now you turn your eyes on yourself, on your loss, on your own broken hopes, you will walk in the shadow, and every other way will seem brighter than yours; every other heart's burden less heavy than your own. But if you turn your eyes away from yourself to God, you will walk in the light, leaving the shadow behind all the way, and seeing, with eyes that tears have made keen, the shadows that fall across someone else's way, and the burden that is breaking another heart. I cannot explain *why* weeping with another dries my own tears, but it does; nor why sharing another's load should make me less conscious of my own, but it does; nor how putting out my hand to save someone else from stumbling in their sorrow keeps my foot from slipping, but it does. It sounds so figurative, but it is so truly *fact*. I long that you should prove it.

There is no answer yet to the cry of your heart: 'Why, O God, why?'; no light that gives promise of dawn; no explanation that makes the seemingly crooked way appear straight: and no answer could bring back what you have lost. No explanation could restore what is gone. But there is a choice left to you— the choice whether your loss shall make your heart narrower or wider, richer or poorer, stronger or weaker, more selfish or more sympathetic—whether your sorrow shall be more a finding than a losing.

I struggle to express this because I want you to choose

the better part; to take the grief God has sent, and let Him make it a blessing. If this is to be, you must stretch out the arms of your faith and accept it from God's own hands. Put from you for ever the dark thought that, if this or that had been, 'my beloved had not died': no blessing or enrichment can come from any death unless this is so. Whether it be the death of a hope or of a love, or of one dearer to me than life itself, there can only be blessing in it when my heart can say, even in its anguish, 'It is the Lord, let Him do what seemeth Him good.'

A doubt, a motion of rebellion, turns the sorrow into a sword that pierces my very soul, and slays every good spirit that could have helped. Then I am alone indeed, in the moment of my greatest need. For to doubt Him drives God away more surely than to hate Him, and to rebel separates me from my Comforter more truly than if I betrayed Him.

And you must go a step further still. It is a step you can take—the step that takes you to the heart of God. You must *trust*. To see God's hand is not enough. It might only be strong to hurt and not to heal. To recognize His providence might only paralyse hope, unless I could still believe Him to be what, in days of joy, I thought He was: believe Him to be all love; believe Him to be all mercy; believe Him to be all wisdom.

Faith is the only soil in which a sorrow planted with bleeding hands and watered by bitter tears could ever spring up to blossom with new hope and joy for you, and to bring forth good fruit abundantly; leaves to heal another's heart, fruit to feed another's hope.

Do you accept this from God? Are you submissive in your own spirit? Does your faith drive back your fears? Do you rest in God's love even while you suffer under His hands?

You *can* believe! You *must* believe! Your faith is to make the difference between light and darkness. Doubt cannot keep your sorrow out, but faith brings God in. Believe—and live—and in the strength of faith go bravely forth to meet others in their griefs, and your faith shall not only save you, but those to whom you go.

One other thing—I am praying for you that you may come to realize, as you have not yet done, that intimate nearness of the Lord Jesus that makes us understand in a new way the beautiful and tender words: 'Surely He hath borne *our* griefs, and carried *our* sorrows.'

I *do* pray for you. It is the one thing I can do. 'Lord Jesus, wrap Thy pity round this heart, shielding it in the storm, and let Thy Presence give strength *now* and all the way.'

My Jesus, as Thou wilt!
　　Oh, may Thy will be mine!
Into Thy hand of love
　　I would my all resign.
Through sorrow or through joy
　　Conduct me as Thine own,
And help me still to say,
　　My Lord, Thy will be done!

My Jesus, as Thou wilt!
　　If loved ones must depart,
Suffer not sorrow's flood
　　To overwhelm my heart,
For they are blest with Thee,
　　Their race and conflict won;
Let me but follow them—
　　My Lord, Thy will be done!

　　　　　Yours in sympathy

15
VOICES OF THE SPRING

APRIL 1915

My Dear G___,

> The weather's gettin' springy,
> An' the birds are gettin' singy.

And it would not do to let the cadets know what a longing I have just now to be away from the Training College.

> Away, away from men and towns
> To the wild wood and the downs!

Can you understand the feeling? It came over me a few days ago with a rush. Suddenly I knew the spring had come. I knew the buds were bursting. I knew the little streams in the meadows were hurrying with cheerful swiftness about their business, singing as they went. The very wind, I felt sure, would be dropping its rough ways and starting already to practise the refreshing and caressing touch that will be all the fashion when it is greeting the delicate new blossoms that will presently make the humpy old fruit trees look like fairies.

And I find myself—the human part of me—hankering after long, long tramps over the common, or by the sea, or through the lanes—anywhere where the smell and the song and the sunshine of the spring will be around me, so that the inspiration of it might sink into my heart and awaken in my spirit a stirring and a moving that will show itself in fresh expressions of the life of my spirit towards God.

How lucky W___ is in her country corps. These privileges of spring can be hers without escaping from her work, without neglecting it even. If only she and I could change places! Then I should arrange a day's visiting in the villages, and all the way there and back I should be listening to the message of the spring. All the living things would have something to say to me, from the lark in the heavens to the leaf in the hedgerow.

If—but it is no use 'if-ing'! It is not my duty to visit villages. You and I are both in the city, from which the sights and songs of spring are far removed. All the same, if you could put your head round the office door just now you would see that spring has come to me in the shape of a bunch of twigs—hawthorn and hazel. They are sitting cheerfully together in a little green mug, and they talk quietly to me every time I look at them. The warmth of the office has coaxed them into leaf, and I should say they look just about what W____'s hedges will look like by the time you see this. I wonder if she will hear and see in her leaves what I hear and see in mine?

As I sit here quietly, the only sound that reaches me is the hum of the trams on the high road, and in the stillness my little group of twigs speak many things. They are faithful messengers, and my heart is ready to hear. As I listen I want to gather and arrange what they say so that I may translate it into words for you; but every time I try, it seems I have been listening to what cannot be translated into words, and I am already wishing I had begun to write you about something else.

I think the first message was one of cheer. All the buds seemed bursting to tell me: 'here is another new beginning!' New buds on the old twigs! As my thoughts have been dwelling much on endings lately, it was reviving to watch even a leaf begin. For you must know that commissioning day is nearly here. The excitement increases. The whole house, cadets and officers, rise at times above the very clouds in joyful anticipation; and at times, as is inevitable, sink into the mighty deeps, anxious and afraid. Always busy, we begin now to be more busy. One result being that this letter to you will have to be written a bit at a time, which will account for its being muddly! But you will have tucked away in some corner of your mind a vision of the TC during those last days, and I know you will not be hard on my attempt.

All goes on much as usual. People of a speculative temperament are in great form just now. There is so much to speculate about! Such a delicious possibility of being right about something, coupled with the fact that, in the excitement, probably no one but yourself will remember you were wrong, if you are! Who will the new sergeants be? Who will be the sergeant-major's lieutenant? Shall the new uniforms be worn to travel in, or shall the second-best be braided? Yellow braid is in great demand at the trade stall. These and weightier problems are being faced, and the pros and cons duly weighed.

Oh, what days! How I hate them! The sense of the end at hand—a putting to the test of so much. I always long to keep the girls, to be able to do a little more to make sure they will be strong—strong to face the enemy, 'and having done all to stand'. But I wonder if a training college officer could ever feel that *all* had been done? Dear girls! May God keep them, and perfect in them all that concerns them. 'He which hath begun a good work in you will perform it.'

How wonderful God's beginnings are! Most wonderful to me in that they come so often, always inviting me to join in with one of my own. Every day is, in this sense, a fresh start. In God's world I seem to understand there is no end without its beginning. The one follows the other. The completion of one duty or loveliness is at the same time the commencement of some other. How is my heart entering into this?

It does me good to pull up and face things in their relation to myself. I am so often facing them for other people. Just now how I am praying and yearning for the girls, that they may embrace the new opportunities that are ahead of them. In a true sense the end of training is for them a beginning—a beginning of responsibility; of battle; a beginning of beginnings! Remember it when you meet them, for beginnings are generally uphill work; and a word, especially a spiritual word, from one who makes them feel that training days are not so far behind as to be quite forgotten, can often accomplish more than you would guess.

I wonder if the new April green will speak to any of them of the responsibilities and hopes of their own new beginnings. I hope so.

My leaves have reminded me, too, of what helps me to finish well—so far as this session goes; that for my work as well as for myself there is the hope of another beginning. Thank God! A chance to do better—to succeed where I seem to have failed; to be more determined, more painstaking, more really earnest and self-sacrificing. And by His help I will.

Will you? You are in a new corps. Shall I send you a few twigs to give you the same message? You see, every spring it is not only that leaves burst out and flowers shoot up where they did before, but that there are more of them—a pushing forth of leaves and twigs in addition to those that appeared last spring. Where one violet lifted its head and looked shyly round alone, this year there are two, or even three.

Oh, that for us it could be so, and that where there had been some faith there might be more—where some self-forgetting, still more—some serving, some loving, some giving, still *more* and STILL MORE! Give me springtime in my soul, O Lord Jesus, that all of Thee in me may spread and multiply.

If you could only see how the leaves have grown, just in one week—there is half an inch difference in the size of some of them and yet the growth goes on so slowly and silently. There is no moment in which I can suddenly point and say they are bigger, and while I watch they do not seem to change.

That teaches me another thing about the working of

the Lord in me, the putting forth of my new leaves—whether it has to do with myself, or through me with my work. I mean this, that the increase is going quietly and steadily on. It is a growth continuing every moment, through every happening and doing of every ordinary day. While there may be some places where I may realize that I *am* growing more than in others, the growing itself must be going on all the time. In the sunshine, in the rain, in the winds, through the things that seem to help, and through the things that seem to hinder. Oh, the comfort of knowing God is working in me: that the spiritual life, the Christ life, in me is growing!

And the best of it is, I know it is so, just in the same way that I know it about my leaves. Though I cannot feel or see them actually growing, I know they are growing by comparing them with what they were. So I know it about my own soul, though at times, I do not *feel* different, nor come to places of sudden change. Yet, as I look back, I see that there has been a growth, and I can say to the honour of the Lord, 'His life in me increases.' I do not find in the past any better experience than I enjoy in the present. This is the best yet! I used to be puzzled when I heard people talk about their *first* love and a simple faith, as of something that they wished they still possessed. I wondered if I should ever feel so. I pray I never shall. Certainly at present, looking back tells me how truly the life of the Spirit is a continual progress.

Dear G____, I hope there is some such response from your heart, and that in these days *you* have the joy of knowing that the fruits of the Spirit abound in your life more than ever before; that, looking back, this spring finds you richer in all spiritual gifts than any spring before it.

How rich we are, not only in what we have, but in the certainty that we can and shall have more; be more; see more! Talk about the gloss wearing off; to me it seems that things shine more and more. My wonder is, not that I should have so slowly recognized that 'all is not gold that glitters', but that I should have passed by so much gold without seeing it glitter!

This is true about my work and the folk about me. Souls are so much more worth helping than I thought—so much more interesting, too. But it is true also of my own experience. I see in Christ more than I ever dreamed I should. I have joy in spiritual things, as real and more real at times, than any earthly joy. And, above all, I have the realization of that quiet working and moving in me of the Holy Spirit my Guide, my Strength, my Comfort. Yes, that is an expression of another line of thought awakened in my mind by my twigs. The life *in* me is the author of every outward expression—the living sap. My poor little messengers will presently droop and die and rot. They are separated from the source of their life. Circumstances keep them apparently growing just now: they seem to flourish, but will soon fade.

Oh, may I take the lesson home to my heart, and you to yours! There can be no lasting life in us apart from a real union with God. 'I am the Vine, ye are the branches. He that abideth in Me, and I in him, the same bringeth forth much fruit.' My little twigs appear so thoroughly alive now; but they are separated from the parent tree, and, for all their gay looks, will soon wither and die.

How easily that might be true of me! What a fading and withering and dying, unless the life of God flows into me continually! How watchfully and jealously must we guard against any plucking away, against any separation from the Living Source! All the more so that it would be for us as it is for my twigs, that the outward things might for a time seem to prosper as before. For the source of spiritual life is hidden just as the sap is. It flows silently through the whole, from root to tip, giving life and making growth possible.

So may the life of Jesus be in you—in me. Then there will be new beginnings, fresh ventures, and more of all that belongs to the Divine. For in the spiritual world, as in the world of nature, the law of life is the law of growth, and the life of God in us must mean that we 'grow up into Him in all things.' His life in all that we are, the seen and the unseen; coming into everything that is a part of us, as the sap flows into everything that is a part of the tree—our thoughts, our words, our deeds. This will mean a renewing and reviving, an increasing and keeping alive the spiritual qualities of faith, love, humility, patience, self-sacrifice, forgiveness, mercy, justice, and truth.

Let us both go on thinking over what the twigs have said, and let us be more daring to make beginnings in some matters, and more trustful as to results: remembering always, even if last time we made the attempt things did not work out as we hoped—at least, perhaps, it did not seem so—it is our privilege to begin again with the spring. We shall meet discouragement in varying forms. The new beginning, the patient working out and working on, is not easy always, 'but God giveth the increase', and that makes every effort worthwhile.

Yes, dear G___, this is the message of the spring to my soul and to yours, 'God giveth the increase'; and so by faith we may claim from Him all the increase of whatever Divine quality we need, to make all that is ours show forth the beauty of His work in us; just as the trees and the grasses are showing forth the perfect grace of His work in them. 'That henceforth our lives may be—beautiful for Thee.'

Yours, to serve

16
PRAYER

MAY 1915

My Dear B____,

I am glad you wrote me just as you were feeling, for, though my knowing does not alter anything, it does make me better able to pray for you, because I understand more what you need. I wish, though, you were not so far away, for a talk over things might probably help us.

You must not be too hard upon yourself. Everything is new, and I remember how naturally impatient you are to see results and know that you are succeeding. But do not forget that if it is true that the Lord is seeking 'hearts to help Him with the reaping', it is as true that He needs the kind of spirit that is prepared to help with the sowing: a spirit that will not faint during the waiting days that often come, in the spiritual world as truly as in the natural, between the sowing and the reaping. Remember, too, that often the best harvests must be waited for the longest! Mustard and cress grow up in days, but the wheat will not be ripe for months.

So be sensible, and while you must go on giving all you have to give, preparing the ground and watering the seed, do not be discouraged because the results do not appear as quickly as you had hoped. You do not want only mustard and cress, though that is not to be despised!

Your last word asks me to pray: I will.

What a mystery prayer is! I wish I understood it better. But I do thank God that the power of it does not depend on being able to explain it, any more than the light in the office depends upon my knowing all about electricity. As long as I carry out certain instructions that I *do* understand, I have the light: so with my praying.

At one time I must confess I spent much time exercising my little mind in the hope of stretching it to a comprehension of the mystery, when I should have profited far more had the same amount of thought and energy been spent in seeking the things my heart was needing—things that could only come to me by prayer.

Now I just leave the mysterious side, and, by carrying out the Bible instructions about prayer, I am entering constantly into a more confident faith in its power; because, as the result of putting it more and more to the test, I am discovering *how much it accomplishes*.

In this way the strength of prayer is increasingly a definite *fact* in my life. So I shall pray for you in connexion with these special circumstances, and know that in some inexplicable way my praying will help.

I hope you are praying yourself as much as you ought, for certainly your *own* praying can do more for you than that of anyone else. In your present difficulties, particularly, the very fact that there is no one to whom you could speak, makes your speaking to God the more essential.

Looking back on my own experience, I can see that my private prayer has come to be of two distinct kinds. The kind of praying I first learned was that definite closing out of all other doings and settling down to pray only. No day can be complete without some such time. I generally find it easier to take it in the evening. I wonder what you find is the best time? The other that grew out of the first. I mean that *life of prayer* which belongs to everything; that spontaneous lifting of the heart to God that becomes the habit of the soul. It would be difficult now to say which is the more precious, or which means the most to me. Both have had to be cultivated.

I cannot honestly say that praying in public or private was at first easy. In fact, it is often difficult even now, and in many ways I am still learning how to pray. God knows how slow some of us are when it comes to this, and He sends all kinds of experiences to teach us.

In how many hearts has prayer been more a form than a life; more the performance of a duty than the expression of a desire, until the spirit of prayer was born in some dark night's struggle, when the soul knew that if it let go without the blessing it was needing, all was lost. At such times the cry still goes up to God, 'I will not let Thee go, except Thou bless me.'

Without doubt, in my own life the darkness of temptation and sorrow has taught me to pray—to wrestle before God until my soul found strength to go up to its Calvary.

Next to the help of such experiences, longing over other souls has done most to teach me how to pray. Both in my corps and later at the Training College, yearning to bring souls into the light, to help them up to what I felt were God's purposes for them, has made me pray just as naturally as being hungry makes you eat. There seems to me to be no such perfect fellowship with the Lord as that which comes when we travail in spirit before Him for the soul of another.

I wonder, B____, if you have realized as fully as you ought the privilege of doing this, and the power of it to help. And, oh, the comfort of it! To feel that your own imperfect efforts to bless souls by word or example can always be supplemented by prayer. Many a time, I am sure, the prayer that has followed or preceded my effort has accomplished more than the effort itself.

Oh, never, never let the devil persuade you that your prayer does not count! It *does*. And no heart need be without the proof of it; but it must be prayer, fervent, persistent, believing!

I think I have told you before that I am seldom helped by feelings in my own religious experience; but the times when I have been especially conscious of the presence and power of God have been chiefly during seasons of prayer for others. These seem to have brought me nearest to the heart of Jesus.

That other sort of praying is to my soul-life, I think, more what breathing is to the body. Do you know what I mean? I hope so, because for you, as for me, it can and ought to be not only an unfailing source of strength, but such a safeguard. However small a place it holds in our lives, there should be nothing about which we do not speak to God. The prayer that is breathed in a moment ensures the kind word, when, without it, the hasty one might so easily have been spoken; courage to act, when, apart from it, an opportunity of witnessing or sowing might have been missed.

Yes, the silent prayer of an instant has preserved the integrity of the heart and saved the soul from the stain of sin again and again. And the strength of that continual communion with God, which becomes so natural that it is more like talking a matter over with one you love, has enabled so great a host of God's own children to be walking with Him in heavenly places, and has kept them in a heavenly spirit, when things round about were very earthly.

Yes, B____, I *do* believe in prayer, and I *will* pray for you. Let us pray for ourselves and for others more and more; always pray, and not faint.

Yours sincerely

17

AN UNTRUE VISION

JUNE 1915

My Dear T____,

A sentence contained in a letter I received yesterday
has been haunting me in a vague way ever since I read it.
This evening, being a little tired, and, in consequence,
probably, also inclined to be depressed, I found that same
sentence assuming quite a burdensome importance. It
was this: 'The work is a bore!' Written by one of my old
girls, it means a good deal more to me, very likely, than it
would from a stranger.

I began wondering how such a change could come—
how it would show itself; and then from that, I thought
of some folk as I knew them, trying to imagine what
would be outwardly visible if such an inward state
existed. And then, my dear, I had a vision of *you!* I said I
was inclined to be depressed, and so perhaps that
explains why, at a time when I am really happy about
you, I should have pictured you in a state which, if it
were a real one, would grieve me deeply.

Why I should tell you of it I hardly know, except that it
impressed itself on me as a possibility, so to be feared,
that I had a sort of feeling that to write you about it might
help to protect you from it.

I saw you—in a corps—fairly well in body; you seemed
cheerful, dressed with your customary neatness,
working moderately; anyway, steadily. In a word, you
looked what you said you were, quite happy on the
whole. *But soul-saving was at a standstill.* And instead of
breaking your heart over it, as I knew you would have
done at one time, you seemed only anxious to prove to
me that it was not your fault. I could see myself
reasoning, inquiring; and hear you answering and
explaining.

The ground was hard. You said the officers before you
had no souls to speak of. Visiting? Yes, oh, yes, you
visited the soldiers; but it was very difficult to make the
visitation a really spiritual effort, the people were so
ignorant. Well, generally now you did not read with
them, though you prayed sometimes. It was difficult to
say how you got out of the way of it. For one thing, the
soldiers were always talking each other down, and you
felt it out of harmony to pray. I must remind myself it

is only an imaginary picture of you. We both believe praying is never out of harmony where a soul is in need.

House to house visitation, you assured me, you really had not time for in this corps; besides, you had taken up a special branch of study—book-keeping, I think it was. You hoped not to stick in the field for ever, and some other qualification might help you to get a change later.

You were rather proud of the scrupulous cleanliness of the little quarters, though you said a few things about the state they were in when you first came. You showed me with some pride the doilies and toilet set edged with rather handsome crochet worked by yourself and lieutenant; but when I asked if you did much sick nursing, you said no, you had found it impracticable, not having time to do it properly without neglecting other work. And I wondered if there were in your care any old soul bedridden, to whom the sight of your fresh face would have been like, almost like, the face of the Son of man, with a power to heal the heart, if not the body. And then I looked at the crochet again. It *was* pretty, and would wear well; perhaps be still in use after some of those old lives had flickered out like a guttered candle.

We discussed the meetings. It was difficult, you said, to get fresh people in, and for that reason you seemed to have given up trying. Open-airs? Yes, if enough soldiers turned up. Oh, no, you and lieutenant seldom stood alone; it rather 'let the Army down', you thought; as bad as marching when there were only five or six of you. You laughed when I reminded you of how you had enjoyed your marches five strong, yourself carrying the flag, and your first convert the drum, in the corps you went to from the Training College. The foolish unwisdom of youth, you said—now you knew better!

As to holiness meetings, your experience was teaching you that the people were too dark spiritually to understand holiness. It was better, you thought, to make the meaning of conversion clear first. A real holiness meeting would be wasted on them. As I listened, I saw the face of our dear old General in Heaven, and those words of his left on record for our guidance came to me: 'If the FO wants his soldiers to fight—to suffer—to conquer—they must be made and kept holy. If the FO is in earnest about this, let him look after his holiness meeting.' Surely, he was a wise soul-winner, and likely to know better than even experience could teach you or me.

Yes, there was a good deal of drinking. One of the corps cadets visited the pubs, but did not sell many papers. You had found pub-booming rather a strain—had not done it at the last two corps; the smoke tried your throat. In fact, on the whole, you had to be rather careful not to go too vigorously at anything. That was why you were always glad of a special, or if any one turned up who could do the meeting.

You wondered how long you would be able to go on—and so we talked, and I watched you, and tried to fathom where the change was. The critical side of you (do you remember my warning you against it in the days of 'personals'?) seemed to have developed. You talked about the soldiers as one knowing every fault and weakness, with but very little hope or sympathy to spare. You dealt hardly with the methods of some officers in the division, notably those you had followed, and you went on to say: 'I'm getting tired of this repetition of hard goes; sometimes the work is a bore!'

I was back to the keynote. My thoughts stopped with a jerk. The sense of depression settling on me lifted. It was *not* true of you. But then came the swift stab of a question—would it ever be so?

Such a change has come, I fear, to some who seemed as safe from it as you are now. How? Why? It perplexes and sometimes almost frightens me. Could it ever creep over my heart? Could I be content in the presence of my people's coldness? Could I be satisfied merely to keep things together when sin is encroaching on all sides; to be sleeping or warming *myself*, like Peter, when the Lord is rejected, despised, forgotten?

I pray sometimes that if I am in such danger, the Lord will smite me with some sudden sorrow or defeat, and so call me back to that place of uttermost need which became in my life the place also of uttermost love—the love of my heart pledged to Him and to His cause among men. Was it not so for you, too? Our love has been because 'He first loved', and in our need succoured us. Shall we be first to stop loving? Or shall we insult Him by keeping up the forms of love after the fire of it has died out? No! Rather let us be praying every day, 'Enlarge, inflame, and fill my heart with boundless charity divine!' And I believe that where our praying about it is real, our living it will be real, too. The impulses of love will move us with pity when we see the people. Love will teach our hands to serve, and even multiply our powers. As it is written of one who so followed Jesus:

> There is no grief nor care of men,
> > Thou dost not own for thine;
> No broken heart thou dost not fill
> > With mercy's oil and wine.
>
> Thy miracles are works of love;
> > Thy greatest is to make
> Room in a day for toils, that weeks
> > In other men would take.

All industries of love wert thou,
  So thoughtful yet so quick—
The angel of the shame-faced poor,
  God's shadow on the sick.

Thou seem'st to have a thousand hands,
  And in each hand a heart;
And all the hearts a precious balm
  Like dew from God impart.

While love so overwhelmed thy days
  With toils beyond compare,
Thy life 'mid all thy countless works
  Was one unbroken prayer.

Whatever comes, let nothing rob you of your love. It is your life—the one thing needful to make your work a joy and not a bore. Love will not be barred by criticism, nor bound by custom. It bursts forth and flows over in new ways every day. It seeks out its ends (never its 'own') with a wisdom and patience that do not recognize failure as such, and finds some new reason for hope in every disappointment.

Love is a light by which you will see a beauty hidden from eyes made blind by self-seeking; the beauty of a soul once broken by sin and healed by the hands of God, even when it dwells in a marred body and with a mind narrowed by ignorance; and, seeing the beauty, love will deal tenderly, being careful because of old scars. The beauty, too, of the young not yet spoiled, but with all the possibilities of a clear, upright life before them: and love, seeing by its own clear light so much further ahead than the young soul itself can see, will be inexhaustibly patient with youth's short-sighted ideas and changing desires, and persuade or compel with a power that is love's own, not less strong because it is always gentle.

Love, too, will light the night of your own heart's weariness when you are alone and tempted; when you have toiled and are slighted; when your flesh is weak, and you *feel* forgotten by God Himself. *Then*, because you love, you will find comfort and strength in the face of the Man of Sorrows, who 'trod the winepress alone'; and while the light of love burns in the heart, no darkness can wholly hide Him.

Pray for love. It is a fire—feed it—fan it. Neglected, it will soon die out. Stir it up by exercise every day. See to it that love *is* the motive behind all you do *now*. Respond quickly to its promptings. Guard it, oh, guard it from the stifling atmosphere of selfishness. Self-seeking will extinguish it before you realize what has happened, and *then* you will be changed, as you were in my picture of you. I think I would rather you left the SA outright! Yes, I think I would.

I know your present corps has its difficulties; but I know, too, that while you keep yourself in the love of God, you will not only do faithfully the duties that are laid upon you, so fulfilling the law ('regulations'); but that, in the strength of the love of Jesus, you will add at every opportunity the self-imposed labours of love, and through all the days fight joyfully because love is in your heart—the love that beareth, believeth, hopeth, endureth *all* things!

Lord Jesus, so let Thy love fill our hearts till it overflows, and keep it so running over that everywhere we go, the souls who touch us may be refreshed, revived, renewed! And may we ever offer Thee with hand and lips a service that is rendered because of the love in our heart.

Thus I pray for myself, T___, and for you.

ps—On reading this over, I notice that it might give the impression I thought crochet and advanced training study were wicked. But you know what I mean. I do not think crochet should ever be done when anything more useful could take its place. For an odd moment that would otherwise be idle, well and good. As to study, here, again, I would say, the people ought to come first.

18

FURLOUGHING DAYS

My Dear P____,

I am pleased to know you are encouraged about your corps. I felt sure there would be good results if you only persevered. Yes, if I am in London when you pass through for your furlough I shall be ever so glad to see you, as you suggest; then you will be able to give me all the news.

As to your furlough, you need it. You ought this year to make it a real rest. I wonder if you have done the best in regard to it in the past? As you have mentioned the matter to me, I am tempted to give you a little advice about it. Will it be any good? I am coming to the conclusion lately, that I am far more ready to give advice than you people to whom I give it are to take it!

Well, to begin with, I would say, make your furlough a *rest*. I rather like the old-fashioned Salvation Army style that spoke of being 'on rest'. I suppose this grew from the fact that in the early days officers did not leave their work unless the need of rest made their absence imperative. In these more organized days of yearly furloughs, I am afraid the 'rest' idea has dropped out rather more than it ought. Whether on furlough, or leading the fight, the aim of the true officer should always be 'first the Kingdom'. To employ our off-duty time in such a manner as to make us unable to return to work as far as possible refreshed and strengthened, is for us not only a folly, but, I think, positively a crime.

Our dear old General used to say his rest was a change of work. There is a sense in which that is true for us all, though not in the same sense in which he meant it. Change is an essential of real rest, and so you should aim at making your few days away from work as much of a change in every way as possible.

We have not yet discovered how to do our work for God on earth without a body! Nobody wants our ghosts merely, and the body has to be taken into partnership in a very serious manner. So, first, I say, rest. Get extra sleep. You know how important I think sleep is—in many cases more than meat and drink. However you may be tempted to the contrary, get off to bed at a reasonably early hour. Even if you do not sleep, the rest will help you to the right kind of sleep when you do get off. Sleep in the evening is much more beneficial than sleep late in the morning; but do both, if you can—and compensate for burning the candle at both ends, as you so often do.

Be in the fresh air as many hours as possible out of the twenty-four. Read, write, sew, and eat out of doors, if you can by any means manage it. Even if the weather be chill and the sun does not greet you warmly, wrap up and be out. It spells life!

Resolutely withdraw your thoughts from the perplexities of the work with which they are always occupied. Your mind cannot be idle, and the only way to rest it is to apply it in some unaccustomed—though not necessarily useless—way. Time for uninterrupted reading is always a luxury as well as a rest. If you do not think so, try it. I will not attempt to advise you as to what you should read, not having any idea as to your taste in that direction; but I would say, do not let all the time be taken up with tales that you only want to forget.

In these days of cheap editions and public libraries good books are within our reach; books dealing with matters likely to be profitable as well as interesting. Such are all histories, whether of nations, societies, or individuals; and, after all, real things are the most interesting.

Rest your mind, too, by allowing it to think its own thoughts. We live in such a rush. All moments of quiet that come are needed for prayer and preparation for meetings; but in these few days let your mind wander with its own thoughts for company, and, like Isaac, go into the fields to meditate. The fields are not the only place for meditation, though some think they are the best. Perhaps this is the most important, for your spirit is your mainspring. All will drag heavily unless your spirit be strong. The annoying part is that the more your spirit needs resting the more difficult it is to rest it, or even to recognize the need.

Do not be surprised if the first days of absence from the rush and strain bring on you a sense of depression. This is just the reaction, and you must help yourself by discouraging thoughts likely to increase that feeling. Let your prayer, for a time, be more praise than petition.

Let your spirit find rest in the thought of God. Creep more intimately near to Him: not by long seasons of prayer necessarily—though opportunities for taking these without the sense of rush and tiredness that are present when in the midst of work are precious—but by many moments of intercourse.

If you are in the country, as I hope you will be, you will find, I think, as I do, a specially hallowed joy in speaking to God in the midst of the works of His hands. To lie on the earth hearing only the voices of nature—the bee, the bird, the breeze in the grasses, and to speak out my heart's need, waiting, unhurried, before the face of that Presence who speaks to me in all manner of secret ways—this is a reviving of spirit, a resting and quieting of the anxious, fratching, and often sorrowful inner man; and if the 'inner' goes back to work renewed, the 'outer' is likely to come up to scratch.

The world is mourning, and all of us are close up to the sorrows of individual hearts; and it is of greater importance than ever that we should be strong and brave and steadfast in faith and love; and if this is to be so our spirits must find strength and rest in God Himself.

The Bible can be so wonderful to you in these days! Do not attempt to be preparing meetings—indirectly you will be getting much—but just be going to it for your own heart only. In the unaccustomed surroundings and doings you will probably find the old words clothed for you with new meaning, and you will gather riches that will be yours when other things that the holiday brought are gone for always.

Without making it a burden, cherish the opportunity for blessing and cheering those with whom you find yourself; particularly if you go to your own people. Days with you mean so much to them. Consider them, and show them by little doings and sayings how truly and dearly you do love them. Let it be a crowding in, so to speak, of the expressions of it that belong to the love of days when you are separated from them.

Read again the instructions on the back of the furlough slip, so simple and yet so wise—so often, I fear, neglected. I do not think I need say to you, remember you are not only a salvationist, but an officer. All the standards you teach and profess belong as much to rest days as to others: so there will be nothing done or said or read unbefitting you as God's minister.

You will not be always in uniform, of course. A change of clothes is good as well as other changes; but your dress will not be worldly, for you have given up the fashions and extravagances of worldly adornment. There should be few occasions when you cannot wear an Army brooch, or something to show whose you are; and whether you do or not, *never allow yourself in any place where you could not go in uniform because the uniform would reproach you for being there.*

It would not hurt you to be away from meetings altogether, or even to go with your own people to chapel (it will make you love the Army all the more); but, certainly, if you do go to the meeting, go in uniform. I know it has so often done real harm when officers have slipped in, thinking no one would notice them. Soldiers naturally do not understand why the uniform is discarded. Full regimentals are certainly not necessary; but you should look like a well-saved soldier, at least.

God be with you in all the days, and give you joy in a realization of His Presence. Without Him thoughts would be dreary company enough just now. How easily we could be swamped by questions to which we can find no answer. The sun shines, the birds sing, the flowers bloom, and *men die!* 'Oh, my soul . . . hope thou in God.' You and I must be stronger in hope. The days demand it. We must turn from the things we do not know to hold the more to the things we *do* know.

That your rest days may help you to this is my hope.

19

RETROSPECT AND PROSPECT

OCTOBER 1915

My Dear L____,

I've been a-journeying,* as you know; have heard and seen much of which I should like to tell you one of these days—much that strengthened my faith and stirred my soul. Now I am back on the old spot. I hear the old sounds and see the old sights. I always experience a sense of comfort when I come back to the familiar, however great may have been the charm of the new; and so you will know it has been good to me to find myself again in the old place, for I *do* love it and my work there.

Although this is perfectly true, there has mingled with my gladness a very different feeling. Usually the beginning of the session is a joyfully hopeful season, but somehow this time I have felt almost a reluctance to gather up the threads and start on the new pattern.

Old questions, long ago satisfactorily answered, have been revived in some strange way, and my spirit has been restless—rather tormented by the thought of the greatness of the work and the smallness of the instrument.

Added to this, the devil has been trying to prove to me by facts (though I ought to remember that even facts often only tell half the truth) that 'making men' according to the pattern is work in which failure often seems more apparent than success. A whole string of incidents from reliable sources—mostly indirectly from the persons concerned—has filtered through to me, each bearing their own little weight of disappointment, and casting their own little share of gloom over the brightness of the opening days.

B____ has broken down in health through her own carelessness; so, instead of being able to carry on her successful work at X____ she is resting. When will some folk learn wisdom? Do *you* remember, or, rather, do you carry out, any of the instructions with regard to your health that you received here?

A____ has gone home, because she could not agree with her captain, and writes to tell me after she has taken the final step.

---

* Journey to Finland for Annual Congress.

C___ has been hampered at every turn by a lieutenant who *will* make personal friends of the soldiers, and talk over corps and quarters matters; and if the captain remonstrates, the lieutenant as good as tells her to mind her own business! How can I cheer up the captain, and not feel a sense that, to have succeeded better in training the lieutenant would have been more to the point than many wise words of advice in face of such a failure?

N___ has been alone fourteen weeks—and I know she is not the sort to be left for one; and E___ who is in her first corps, has not received a word of advice or encouragement from the DHQ since she left the Training College. What is the use of caring so much to help the girls in here when it seems that there are so few who care about helping them outside?

F___ writes me that she has lost her love for prayer, and knows she is losing ground, and is so disappointed with herself. 'Would it not be more honourable to give up altogether?' she writes. How can I help her merely by writing?

G___ informs one of last year's lasses that what they teach you in the Training College is all very well, but it cannot be carried out. Well, if so, what a fool I must be to go on teaching it!

And so the string lengthens out, and in spite of it, here we are beginning again the old lessons, the same exhortations, wrestling to lead the soul up to the standard of holiness and devotion. The fresh young faces look hopefully towards me as I step on to the platform, and the tramping of the feet past the office window tells me they are striding bravely out to face the battles that lie ahead.

One of these days I shall write you a long letter all about the different things the tramping feet say to me, but today I am thinking of the feet that are not 'in the way' as they once were. They have halted; this or that or the other has happened, and they are changed from what they were when they walked by faith and love in and out of the Training College gates. Changed—and not for the better! Why should it be? Did I fail in my duty to them when I had the chance to help? I remember your letter to me a week or so ago in which you say, 'Why are we not doing better here? Is there anything wrong in me?' After all, though you are in the field, and I am still at the Training College, our perplexities spring from much the same root. Perhaps no real lover of souls has ever escaped the darkness of this kind of disappointment—*the disappointment of failing to make people what we want them to be, and what we felt it was in them to be.*

Dear L___, shall we, because of this, give up struggling to bring the souls in our care up to the standard? I have just been asking myself that. Rather ought not every token of past failure to spur us to a new effort?

And here, in noisy old Clapton, in the midst of all the rush of work, has come the vision of the wide, wild forests of Finland, and its still, silver lakes; and their message to me, being interpreted, is this: *God knows how to make yesterday's failure the secret of today's success*. It is so in the forest. All the faded leaves and broken branches of the past help to make the tender green and new shoots of the present. And again, *all that is complete in beauty and service grew from that which was once not complete in appearance or use*. The strong, straight, red-trunked pine was once a sapling leaning to every wind that blew. The clear, still waters in which the heavens are reflected were, in earlier days, restless muddy drops.

And still again, *the sufferings of today will somehow become the glory of tomorrow*. The scar that seems only to disfigure may be the crowning touch of beauty to the whole. The great boulder of rugged grey rock hurled into the bed of the brook, breaks the waters into a spray, and, covered with moss and ferns, its softened outline makes the chief beauty of the nook.

But for all these works God takes time. He is so working in the spiritual world—your world—my world—without ceasing; and who shall be wise enough to know what shall be in the end while we are still in His hands?

So to you there, and to me here, the trees and mosses and waters speak of patience and hope, of hope and patience. For we, working only in the present, have no right to judge tomorrow by today. Only, may God teach us not to let today's failure rob tomorrow, but rather let there be in us the true proof of our righteousness that, though we fail seven times, we try again (Proverbs 24:16). For in God's sight, surely, whether in our own experiences or in our work, the real grief is *not the failure itself, but the disposition on our part to accept it as irretrievable*. We must still reach after the highest, and we shall prove God is able to teach us as much from our failures as from our successes. But to accept failure without renewed effort is to turn it into a shame and a hindrance.

May God guard us from expecting of the sapling the strength of the full-grown tree, or from ceasing to work for perfection because it cannot be produced in us or in others in a day, a session, or an appointment.

May God teach us that He calls us to suffer only that He may add a joy; that He thrusts in the unexpected obstacle so that we may seek and find a new grace. May God teach us that all these truths are the comfort of the believing heart alone. Walking in the blindness of faith and by the ever new strength of love, such a heart can wait God's time, knowing well that 'one day is with the Lord as a thousand years'.

My business and yours is to make the most, whether of the day or the year, working faithfully in the present; trusting God to make the past fruitful, and to bring to perfection all our works for His Kingdom in His own time.

God bless you with an increase of patience and hope.

20
CONCERNING YOU AND YOUR CAPTAIN

NOVEMBER 1915

My Dear N____,

I do not want you to think I do not realize how difficult you find it to be the model lieutenant you set out to be when you left the Training College. It is always difficult to live up to an ideal; but that is no reason why one should give up trying, is it?

My feeling is that, in many respects, it is often harder to be a good second than a good first; and certainly you are more likely to make a good captain (and I expect you to, some day) if you have first proved yourself a good lieutenant. In every circumstance you should seek that double end: first, to be at the moment the very best possible help to your captain; and secondly, to learn how to deal with similar matters on some future occasion when you may be the captain instead of the lieutenant. You may learn—whichever way things turn—from failure, how to avoid failure; and from success, how to succeed. However, for the moment I am most concerned that you should be a good second.

Do you accept your position as such from the Lord? That is the first point to be clearly settled. If in your heart there lurks the feeling that you might have been promoted, or that your lieutenancy is only something to be got through as quickly as possible, you will certainly never see in it what God wants to show you. How can your heart be at rest without the assurance that you *are* in God's hands, and that He is directing for you? I know you had that kind of confidence in Him once. Have you lost it? Make your heart answer if you have; then pray your way back to the possession of it, or you will soon be losing much else.

One of your first duties as lieutenant is to associate yourself in the minds of all the people as the captain's 'man'. You know what I mean. There should be nothing said, or implied, or done, that could make the folk feel that you did not approve of the captain's action. I know you may not always approve. That is, I know you of old as likely to feel now and then that *your* way is better than the way of any one else. Well, so it may be; but as a lieutenant, you are not called on to prove it; or even to express that opinion unless asked to by the captain. Of course, I have not now in mind any question of principle—right and wrong. I know your captain is a good woman.

The lieutenant should loyally carry out the captain's plans. Give them a jolly good try, as honestly and wholeheartedly as if they were your own. As a result, you will find—perhaps to your surprise—that now and then other folk *do* know better than you! (I still tease sometimes, you see.) You and the captain must show an undivided front to the enemy. Earn for yourself from the captain that confidence which shall make her feel she can trust you as surely in her absence as in her presence, to say and do what you feel will most strengthen her position with the people.

If you really feel that a mistake has been made, find a suitable occasion to say so tactfully when you are alone together.

As to your attitude to each other personally, do believe me, the secret lies in the little things. Thoughtfulness, carefulness in small matters that are *not* beyond your reach, will do more to show that you want to help than anything you say. Let what you profess be worked out in fact. Put your comrade's interests and comfort first. She will soon appreciate you, and if she does not, well, the Lord will bless: 'for God is not unrighteous to forget your work and labour of love, which ye have showed toward His name, in that ye have ministered to the saints, and do minister.'

Take the responsibility in the smaller things as far as ever you can. Do not wait to be asked or told—offer! More than ever I see how precious in the world is the spirit of volunteering; and the lieutenant who volunteers, and makes good her offer by action, will be worth to any captain or corps ten times as much as the lieutenant who only does what she is told, or what the 'regulations' require.

Self-discipline *is* so good for you, and now is your opportunity. Do what you do not like doing in such a way that your captain cannot tell but that you are enjoying it! I know how some things will irritate you; but that gives you the chance of mastering yourself, which is what you need to learn, perhaps, more than anything.

After all, you will not be a lieutenant for ever! How small-minded and selfish to want your way, and make a fuss about details that have no real significance! I am anxious about you, and I do want you to take notice of what I am saying.

Sometimes you may be blamed when you are not at fault. Well, you can bear that, if you *know* you have done your best; but let nothing prevent your striving every day to be 'blameless'. The Blessing will come to you in the effort while you are offering all to God. If you really please God, you will most likely please the captain also. To be talking about wanting to please the Lord, and not be trying your best to make your comrade happy, and to serve and help her, is simply humbug! You see I am getting quite fierce.

Remember always, you have *promised*, and *are trusted*, to put the interests of the people first. Now sometimes you may serve them indirectly through the captain. You help her, and because of your help she is better able in her turn to help them. Your spirit of willingness and courage cheers her, and she is able to go to the meeting or to tackle the problem cheerfully and hopefully as a result. In this way your life may be even more fruitful than it would be were all your time and effort expended in carrying out your own plans.

How many a good lieutenant of only moderate ability has had a share in the work and success of a capable and gifted leader who might not have exercised so far-reaching an influence but for the faithful help of the second-in-command. On the other hand, how often the work of the Lord has been preserved when in the hands of an unfaithful leader, by the spirit of sacrifice and devotion in the lieutenant. The history of great advances in all spheres proves that success has had to do with the helper almost, if not quite, as much as with the leader. The leadership of Bible days proves it. The leadership of the Army in our own day proves it. And that you will prove it again, is the hope of,

Yours sincerely

21

THE VISION OF CHRISTMAS

DECEMBER 1915

My Dear Q____,

I do not know how to wish you a happy Christmas! Indeed, I never before felt so 'un-Christmassy', if you can understand such an ugly word. Christmas! The sweet, simple picture of the Child in its Mother's arms, and the old men worshipping a Spirit that was to make all things new. It has been beautiful to revive it all, year after year, and seek to find in it some fresh beauty, some new hope. But this year!

Another picture seems more in keeping with my thoughts, one over which the sweet hopefulness of Bethlehem only casts a deeper shadow. Calvary! The bleak hillside—the crowd of angry faces—man eager to kill—the King whose Kingdom could not be won by the sword—the Man who could bless His enemies—the Saviour who loved the *whole* world.

To me it seems the world has stopped at Calvary, not to repent, but to cry again, 'Away with Him!' Surely, He, looking on the world's anger and anguish, still cries: 'They know not what they do.' To me it is a melancholy thought that, only after the hateful spirit of greed and anger is glutted with the blood and death of the young, having everywhere broken the hearts of women, and robbed childhood of its rights—only *after* this, men will turn again to the message of Christmas, regretting the violence of Calvary, as the world has done before.

Yet, surely, just because the world *is* so blind to the vision of Christ, loving darkness rather than light—so deaf to the message of peace and goodwill; surely, just because this is so, we who have seen, who have heard, need to look again and to listen again, lest the night of unbelief blot from our view the Christ; lest the contradictions of earthly voices drown the heavenly message. If we look and listen for the Divine, even in these days, we shall see and hear more clearly than ever, and Christmas will help us.

Yes, in spite of all this dismal rigmarole, I know I need all that Christmas means—so do you. Thank God for Christmas! What would life mean just now without Bethlehem and all that followed the angels' message? So I say: 'Bless the Lord, O my soul, for the message that rings above the din of a hundred battlefields! Bless the Lord, O my soul, for the Man whose life interpreted the message so that my heart might receive it in all its simple truth. Bless the Lord, O my soul, for the Divine Saviour who brought me deliverance from sin's bondage, that I might live out the message.'

We cannot compel all hearts to accept Christ's gospel. One heart we *can* answer for, and then live so that as many others as we can reach shall see a beauty in Him through us, and so desire Him. This is the only way men can be saved—by seeing goodness and loving it. Then God meets them, whoever they are; and who seeks, finds; who hungers, is filled. Man's condemnation has ever come upon him when he has loved darkness rather than light; when he has seen the good, and chosen the evil.

How can we tell but that the darkness of these days may be doing more than we know to turn men's hearts to the Light of the World and His gospel of peace and goodwill? It may or may not be so, but there is no doubt whatever that the world's greatest need, as well as the greatest need of the individual heart, is to 'see Jesus'. So Q___, dear, must it not be our greatest responsibility, as well as privilege, to make Him manifest?

Wonderful words we have sung and prayed together:

> Make me a blazing fire
> Where'er I go;
> That to a dying world
> *Thee I may show.*

Yes, this is our aim in these Christmas days—in all the days—and if others are to see Jesus in us, we must 'see Him' all the time. The clearness of our vision will decide our likeness to the Model; 'and in the battle's blazing heat, when flesh and blood would quail,' we shall endure, seeing Him who is invisible.

Hell itself cannot prevail over the soul who follows Jesus closely enough to keep Him in view all the time; and while He is the light of our eyes, we shall be brave to look on earth's sorrows, and by faith we shall be seeing clearly 'what worldly eyes cannot behold'—men's sins, their needs; and seeing, too, what is within our reach to do for them. And oh, if one day He shall say to us, 'ye did it unto Me', with what astonished joy we shall say, 'Lord, when saw we Thee?'

There is so much that we had hoped, and still hope, to see, that we do not see yet. God only knows how much. 'But we see Jesus', and while we keep our vision of Him, of His love, His courage, His patience, His humility, we shall not faint.

God give you a Christmas blessing, and all through the New Year in every daily circumstance may you and I 'see Jesus'.

22

A FULL SALVATION—JUST NOW

My Dear C____,

By the time you see this the old year will be finished and we shall have entered into the new. It depresses me rather to realize how quickly the time is flying. How soon, at this rate, all will be over—life ended, and the things that could have been done so far as I and the earth are concerned, for ever undone.

Yesterday evening I was sitting thinking, at the end of the day—of the week—of the year—and, from the happenings of that day and week, my thoughts went wandering back and back.

Sometimes, in a strange, unaccountable fashion, my mind seems to disengage itself from the present, and, even against my will, I am carried to the pleasant places of my childhood. So pleasant, indeed, that I do not go willingly, because coming back to 'now' is like waking up feeling famished just as you were dreaming you were being fed!

Perhaps it is the surest token of a happy childhood that, above everything in life, I should choose to live it over again. Joys, the very thought of which makes my heart beat quicker, leaping over the wet grass in a spring wind, all of us on imaginary prancing horses—for, thank God, mine was not a lonely childhood, nor one spent in the company of other people's brothers and sisters, I was rich in my own—taking the ditches with a thrill that was the more delicious in proportion as the danger of jumping short and landing *in* was real. Who would let the thought of boots and frocks to be brushed and dried—for if they were past a certain stage of muddiness we had to get the dirt off ourselves—burden such a lightheartedness as we felt in the woods and fields?

The winter evenings, with the little crowd sitting on stools round our mother's knee while she read, when everybody must be within her reach if it could be managed, so that as her hand went straying from one to another, each of us should feel it rest on our head, stroking the hair with a touch that is like nothing else in the whole world.

My father's voice at prayers—but I must not go on, the tears that will come are part of the price that makes the luxury of such thoughts prohibitive. Tears for a past joy do not bring it back, and they often unfit one for present joys or duties.

But last night my thoughts did not cluster round such scenes. I was pondering over the places that stand out so far as my spiritual life is concerned, arriving presently at the place where the Blessing of a Clean Heart came to me. So wonderful to look back on, especially when I realize that at the time I did not know it was the Blessing I was seeking. I thought I had it! Still, that mistake did not prevent my entering in.

I saw again the place—all the surrounding circumstances were there like the frame to the picture in my mind. I seem always to be able to see myself kneeling; though at the actual time of my dealing with God I was not kneeling, except in spirit. I remembered the months of controversy and anguish of spirit leading to those moments of action. I saw myself on my knees by the hour, yet defeated again and again, until I began to wonder what good was praying.

Then came this place of uttermost surrender. It was, after all, so simple. I see now, looking back, how I had stumbled at its simplicity; and yet, it is not only a difficulty to understand that makes things hard to do.

I had consecrated all to God. I had ceased to consider myself. I did long to be used for souls; but there were still two things that had barred the way to perfect victory and made my prayers of little use—unbelief and self-will. The first, and perhaps greater step, brought me to the place of the absolute committal of my faith to God. I chose Him as God. I said, 'I will, I do trust Thee'; and from that moment I knew that to allow a doubt would mean a going back from my side of the contract. Whether or not He would ever vouchsafe me any feelings, signs, or other manifestations, I was from that moment pledged to believe God, and to act as though I believed.

The next step meant the renouncing then and for always my right to choose. I said, 'Thy will be done now in what I know, and in the things that are still hidden, and for always.'

Faith made the yielding up of my will possible, and I promised God that if He would in His own way make me able to recognize what was His will for me, I should have no other choice, and when the way of the Lord seemed impossible, faith should enable me to step out in obedience.

The Blessing still means just that: an all-embracing confidence in God, an everyday renouncing of my right to choose in anything, apart from Him. All that had belonged to my spiritual life was so dwarfed and poor, as compared to all that has belonged to it since then; and yet at the time I felt no different, and for long after the change was so gradual that sometimes it was hard to convince myself that all was well. But some things were settled for ever. I knew then what my part was, and it was done.

And so my thoughts came slowly back over the years since, to this year, this day; and exactly why, I do not know, but I challenged my own heart to assure me that I was still living up to my side of the covenant. Was I? Did the experience mean all to me now that it meant then? Understanding it better, did I realize it as fully?

Oh, the joy of knowing the answer quickly; of feeling my spirit respond with joy! So much has changed, so many things have been in my life that I never could have expected; but this assurance is still there, and has been all the way. There is *now* no condemnation. I am *now* fully in God's will. I do *now* trust Him for all.

As I have said to you before, feelings have not helped me much with my religion. But last night I had a feeling of inward joy that had nothing to do with being happy—I was not particularly happy—a joy, that I felt was as the pearl of great price, a possession which would go into the new year with me, *mine*, of which neither the devil himself, nor any change of season or place, can rob me.

That sense of joy was like new strength, and I went to my bed rested in spirit, deciding I would write you about it. You have had the Blessing of a Clean Heart, too. I remember when you claimed it, and, in the hope that the joy of possession may fill your heart as it filled mine, I challenge you! Are *you* living up to all you promised when you claimed it from God's hand? Does the experience mean all to you, and more than, it meant then? Understanding it better, do you realize it fully now?

Dear C____, do you? If so, write and tell me, and let us rejoice together. The new year probably holds much we do not expect, but if we keep through the untrodden ways an unstained heart, whatever our work may be, the Lord will be glorified in us, and we shall have had, if we are spared, another year, walking with Jesus every day.

In this matter let us be continually faithful with ourselves. Let the very failures we see in others be a perpetual call to our own hearts. The world more than ever needs to see Christ, the Holy One, in us who bear His name. This was the purpose of the Father's love that sent Him. At the Home Lodge breakfast table this morning I was reading the verses: 'That we, being delivered out of the hand of our enemies, might serve Him without fear, in holiness and righteousness before Him all the days.'

All the days! Yes, all the days of this year walking

with Jesus in white. Thank you, dear Lord, for such a hope!

Peace be with you, my dear girl. Peace within, and plenty of fighting the devil without! What better new year's wish for a salvationist?

Yours, in peace or war

23

KEEPING A FULL SALVATION

FEBRUARY 1916

My Dear C____,

When I was writing to you last, there seemed so much I wanted to say for which I had neither time nor space. The result is, I am tempted to send you a further edition. I realize, I think, more clearly than ever, that if we are to have the assurance of God's help in our efforts, all activities in our service for Him must spring from a heart kept clean. It seems to me that the great objective of the devil's attack upon us is to rob us of the possession of this clear relationship between God and our own spirit.

How easy to become cumbered with the 'many things'; and to forget that, before we can really hope to cope satisfactorily with them, we must make sure of an uninterrupted communion with the Lord, who is to be our strength and wisdom in these very matters.

The other day, as I was sitting over the fire in the office, talking to one of the girls about the Blessing, she broke into something I was saying with these words: 'But, Major, it's not now only, it's keeping it!' She was right. Keeping it is a vital point. What is the use of an experience, however beautiful, that we cannot keep?

I suppose you, as well as I, remember times when the fear of some failure in the future prevented our action in the present. For a time, perhaps, we dared not claim the Blessing, because to keep it looked so impossible. And in those first days and months of holy living, we watched and guarded the gates of our souls that no enemy should rob us of the precious possession within. I wonder how far that fear of losing it is still present with us? Be that as it may, I am sure that in proportion as our experience is precious to us, we shall watch and guard and pray without ceasing.

The words I referred to just now were spoken by a soul hesitating before the greatness of that act of absolute surrender. I tried to give the help that love and prayer and faith teaches one heart to give another, showing that the same attitude on our part that made us able to receive the Blessing could ensure its continuing in our possession.

That was some days ago now, but the words have since come back to me—'It's keeping it!' A morning or two

after, at Home Lodge prayers, we were singing the song
in which are the lines—

> Why wilt Thou not for all my life
> My helpless soul defend;
> And bear me through the doubtful strife,
> And keep me to the end?

I looked round at the faces gathered about me. I saw in
them the expression of the earnest hope of each heart.
Faith cried—'Why not? Why not all of them kept to the
end—kept fighting; kept faithful; above all, kept
sanctified?' Even the devil cannot find a sufficient
answer. There need be no reason why not; and yet I
realized while we were singing, how persistently the
powers of evil would work, using every manner of means
to rob the individual soul of the abiding witness of God's
favour.

It seems no use, my dear C____, to try to write to you
all I feel. It is so hard to put into words the intimate
things of the soul. And yet we must try, because to us has
come the responsibility of helping others, and if *we* do
not learn how to speak of these matters, who will?

I wonder if you are doing as much as you might in this
matter? I mean helping souls with whom you come in
contact, by a willingness to talk to them of spiritual
things.

So many seem to fail to keep a victorious experience,
to lose hold, really from *not knowing how* to keep hold,
as much as anything. It is far, far more important that
souls should be taught how to keep in the way than that
they should be helped back into the way. For one thing,
it is so much more difficult to regain a lost experience. If,
after once having enjoyed the certainty of God's favour
as the result of steadfast faith and loving obedience, the
soul is from any cause again in the uncertainty of
unbelief, and under the cloud of condemnation, it finds
the way back to the simplicities of faith and submission
very hard—so hard as to be only understood by those
who have passed through the experience, or have seen
others struggling in it.

Realizing this, I feel that a tremendous responsibility
devolves upon us to see that in all our efforts to bring
people into the joy of possession, there should be no
failure on our part to make as clear as possible what is
required in order to 'keep it'.

Judging from your own experience and from that of
others, I wonder what you would say is the most
important? I wish when you write me, you would
sometimes express your own judgment about things a
little more definitely. I have a great idea that if we
exchanged opinions more freely with our comrades, we

should learn a great many things that would teach us the ways of the Spirit.

I think, on this matter, I should put first—*cultivating a spirit of prayer*. In my own experience the fear of going back on the promises I made to the Lord (to which I referred in my last letter to you) taught me in a practical way what it means to pray without ceasing; and praying that I might not lose what I had, taught me how to pray my way into new victories and up to higher standards. I am sure that many of our people, especially our younger people, find themselves in circumstances of temptation and difficulty into which they would never have entered had their praying been properly associated with all the doings and thinkings of their lives.

While I realize the danger of saying anything that looks like under-estimating the importance of set times and places for prayer, I think that perhaps in our anxiety to avoid doing that, we do not say enough as to the helping power, literally the keeping power, of constant prayer.

When I am tempted—as I sometimes am, I can assure you—to greet with real impatience the hundred and twenty-first interruption that comes in a morning's work, the very expression of desire involved in a prayer for patience strengthens me against the temptation, even apart from any answer to the prayer.

Then certainly equal with, if not before, prayer I should put *the importance of the repeated assertion of our faith*. For me, this is so, perhaps, because the fiercest temptations have associated themselves with attacks on my faith. Yet, how many times has a speaking out to my own heart of my definite promise to trust God intensified my consciousness that, at any cost, I could not afford to yield one inch of ground to the enemy of souls; and that, feelings or no feelings, I must hold my heart to a faithful standing by its covenant.

The same thing has helped in another way— *reminding myself that I counted on the Lord*, even in things that *could be done apart from Him*. Learning to trust Him where I was not really conscious of my need of Him, helped me to trust Him where I seemed conscious of nothing but my need.

Faith, it seems to me, is to the sanctified soul vanguard and rearguard. Sometimes the battle rages ahead, and it is only by faith that we storm the enemy's strongholds. Sometimes we need the protection of our faith after the battle is over, when the temptation is to doubt results, or God's wisdom, or our own discretion with regard to things that are past. But faith protects us every time. The pillar of cloud goes before, making victory possible, standing between us and the enemy;

making us able to know, as Isaiah says: 'my work is with my God.' There is no doubt about it if, in the first place, we did it with Him, whether it were great or small.

There are hosts of things in these days to turn our hearts and minds easily enough from this simple, everyday faith in God; but can anything be to the soul such a strength?

Thinking of the special difficulties of these present days, I am glad for myself that the Lord showed me that 'keeping it' would involve 'avoiding vain questions'. There are plenty of them about; vain, chiefly in the sense that there are no answers to be found! But whether I have thought I could find an answer or not, I know that they are forbidden ground. I cannot risk what it cost so much to win. After all, we are busy enough with problems that need dealing with, and ought to be content to wait until the atmosphere of a new world enables us to grasp the mysteries of the ways of God by the light of His own Presence. Until then we may dwell in peace, for we possess—

> Jesus, a Saviour born to save:
> To save at night, at noon, at morn.
>   To keep:
> To keep from sin, from doubt, from fear.
> To keep, for lo! the Keeper's here.

God keep you!

24

A PARABLE OF PAVING STONES

MARCH 1916

My Dear V____,

It is just pouring with rain. The streets are silent but for the splashing of the drops as they bear down upon the pavements, and the sighing of the wind as it swings round the corner of the house.

What a difference between those sounds and the soft, soaking whispers of the rain as it falls among the leaves and grasses; where every little blade and all the baby buds try to outreach each other in their eagerness to welcome the life-reviving waters; where the wind makes music among the yielding boughs like the sound of the sea waves playing with the pebbles on the shore in summer. It is only when the trees are unyielding that the wilder music of the storm is spoiled by the crack of the stiff-necked among them.

I suppose the pavements are composed of a kind of earth that perhaps at some earlier stage in its existence was soft and fruitful. Then, the rain found a welcome; and the soil drank in the showers gratefully, and was enriched by the quickened growth which followed.

Now, the pavement hides no living germs, and the rain falls only to splash unwanted on its hard and unresponsive face. I can hear the water now hurrying down a gutter grating in a bubbling scurry to find a place where there is a chance of doing some good; for what use is a raindrop from the skies to the pavement that only rolls it off into the gutter? And how can the wind of heaven produce anything but a moan out of the unbending front of a brick wall?

And the moral of that is—do not turn into a paving stone or a brick! Which, being interpreted means, keep your heart tender, even if it hurts more when it gets trampled on; and do not get so confirmed in your way of doing things that you fail to yield to the impulse of the Spirit which 'bloweth where it listeth'.

I am not familiar with the process that produces paving stones, but I do know a little of the way hearts become stony. It is painful, yet true, that our work itself would have that result if we let it.

Nothing has a more hardening effect on human nature than the constant repetition of anything. And is not life made up of repetitions? Mine is. However interesting and important the matter in hand may be, the fact that we have done it fifty times before, and expect to do it fifty times again, tends to take off the edge of what we feel about it; and so, many *feel* less, and go on feeling less, till they reach the 'pavement' or 'brick wall' stage, and feel nothing! It is true they get through a good many things very easily as a result. They require little or no preparation for the meetings. They do not feel the responsibility. They hardly worry over anything, unless it be that they cannot take more care of themselves. The sins and sorrows of the people barely hurt *them* at all. They see all unmoved, and go through the routine of corps or office duties in the 'mechanical' manner so ably described in one of the Training College lectures, long ago forgotten by you.

In a way, I am sorry for those who have reached that stage, or are on the way to it. They miss so much that is good. God sends rain from heaven, and it simply rolls off into the gutter! Did you ever sit by 'paving stones' in a meeting? If they take the trouble to sing, their thoughts are far away. Songs cannot stir them as they once did. They criticize the speaker, and can find nothing that fits *them* in what is said. They never pray aloud, unless called on; would, in fact, almost as soon miss the meeting as be present. They sometimes eat sweets and write notes, while—but my illustration is getting all in a muddle! You see what a chaos my mind must be in when it comes to talking of paving stones eating sweets! Still, in spite of that, do you recognize the class?

Whatever changes may come over you, my dear V____, please do not become a 'paving stone'. Now, you are true, brown earth, holding all sorts of surprises for yourself and others. Many things may spring up in you that will be a joy to you and to me, as well as to those who will look to you for help and inspiration. Now, even in the most ordinary meeting you are blessed, and your thirsty soul drinks in refreshment from the oldest songs and the simplest prayers.

A ray of sunshine in the morning; the smile of the sick child you have gathered in your arms; the hesitating prayer of the newly saved; the friendly patronage of the world's disreputables; such everyday things as these come to you with a sweet freshness that brings laughter or tears, or both; and, passing, leave you with a spirit blessed and inspired for the heat of the day's battle. Such little things as these—have you not found it so?—water the tender heart. The result is, you are growing all kinds of new graces, and supply an increasing number of folk with the flowers of your sympathy and the fruits of your loving service. Please go on being like that!

You may sometimes be hurt by other people's criticism, but do not harden your heart by beginning to criticize. You may be thought old-fashioned and soft, and be told that it is time you lost your illusions, and faced things as they are. As a matter of fact, the people who *feel* generally get the truest view of men and things. You ought to begin to 'stand up for your rights', they say. It is emotional to shed tears over sinners, and folly to get excited and work so hard—in short, it is time you were a 'paving stone'.

Let them air their opinions. They may be wise in the sense the world recognizes wisdom, but do not follow their advice nor their example. You may suffer more often, but you are richer every day, and blessings received from the hand of the Lord shall quicken your spirit to a fuller life.

Worldly wisdom turns men's hearts to stone whether inside the Salvation Army or outside; but heavenly wisdom, which is to the world foolishness, makes the spirit of a man more and more like the spirit of a little child—tender, trustful, transparent. Your brother man may wound your tender soul, may betray your trustfulness, may ridicule your simple honesty; but the God of Heaven will wrap you in His comfort, trust you with His work, and reveal to you His secrets.

Let us pray for this. Let us watch for this. Let us work for this every day: that our hearts may be kept tender, trustful, true, toward God and man; that the rain God sends 'on the just and on the unjust' may find its way to the roots of every spiritual quality in us; that love and faith and humility may thrive and flourish; that our wills may bend to every holy wind of inspiration. So shall the music of praise to God not cease while His Spirit moves in us, and no rebellion shall spoil the sweet harmony of life.

No, V____, do not be a 'paving stone'! Keep as soft and tender as you possibly can, and I do not think the Lord will let you be short of rain.

Yours, serving

25
WHY WEAR UNIFORM?

APRIL 1916

My Dear X____,

The question is one upon which I fear you did not really form an independent opinion when you were here, or you would not now be so much influenced by what others do. In this, as in all other things, is it not important that we should set up a standard of our own, and not be ready to lower it to match that of anyone else?

I wonder if the matter has had your thoughtful attention. It seems to you at the moment, perhaps, a little thing, but it may have much to do with your influence. To me it has always been a much wider question than that of conforming to Salvation Army custom or regulation. The wearing of uniform is to me the result of accepting certain principles. If this were so for all who wear uniform, we should never have known that strangest of mixtures—the uniformed Salvation soldier who may be seen on a week-night dressed in harmony with the latest fashions, and even wearing furs and feathers!

The uniform has a multitude of good points about which you and I fully agree, I believe. I wonder how far we are in harmony when it comes to the underlying principles?

Would you not say the uniform is, in the first place, a witnessing for God? From the scrap of ribbon you pin in your latest convert's coat to the full regalia of the officer, it is intended that it should be a testimony in favour of Jesus Christ. If so, how important that with all we say to encourage people to wear uniform we should impress upon them the responsibility of acting up to it every time.

If you agree that this is so, is your query not answered? Surely, there can be no question as to whether a soldier of Jesus should want to witness for Him as constantly as possible or not. Therefore, at such times when full uniform is not suitable, the real salvationist will be glad to wear a little badge or brooch or ribbon.

I quite realize that when you are on furlough you may not want to be always in full uniform, and marked out as an officer, but I cannot see why you should want to hide the fact that you are a salvationist.

Then, did it not mean to you a definite sign of separation from the world and worldliness? I am as puzzled as you are as to the people who alternate with uniform dress that differs little from the fashions of the world. But we are not in the world to judge the world, or anyone in it. There is, however, no doubt as to our responsibility for ourselves, and you ought not in this matter, *or any other*, to regulate your conduct merely by the doings of others.

Did you renounce the world, and, in the words of our dear General and Founder, decide that 'in all these things', i.e., dress, etc., 'the rule of simplicity should be followed, and nothing should be done for vain glory, or in conformity to the changing fashions of the world'?

If the Salvation Army could, by some evil magic, disappear from the face of the earth tomorrow, and there were no regulations and no one to write you long-winded letters—is there such a thing?—would there be left in your mind any conviction on this matter of clothing the body?

In all ages it has seemed fitting to people that those set apart for the service of God should be distinguished from their fellows by some special dress; and in most cases the original idea was that such an outward sign would show a contempt for, and a desire to be separate from, the spirit of display so universally shown in the dress of the day. It would be interesting could we discover how much adherence to such a distinction in dress has had to do with maintaining the definite characteristics of various religious bodies, and how far a persistence in the use of this outward sign of separation would have delayed the decline of spiritual vigour and activity in some societies. I cannot tell; but I am sure of this—that the Salvation Army was called into being by God to be, amongst other things, a protest against the spirit of worldly display in Christians; and if, in the adornment of our bodies or our homes, our example ceases to be a protest, I for one feel we shall be failing to fulfil one of the reasons for our existence.

Because of this conviction, I grieve to see, as I did in you the other day, those little signs that you are taking thought to decorate yourself. There need not be a gale in order to tell which way the wind blows, and even the arrangement of the hair and the tying of a bow may indicate a certain attitude of mind.

It seems to me that to wear uniform because one must, and to plunge into worldly 'private' the moment one may, reveals a state of mind and heart very different from that of those men and women who won for us the inheritance of the confidence of the people, and the opportunity to serve them that we are now enjoying.

If Paul was willing to be a vegetarian all his life rather than hinder a weak brother, how much more easily should we be able to leave alone any ornament or decoration that might identify us with the unsanctified, or tend to lessen the distinction between the salvationist and the worldling.

I wish the Lord had clothed us in fur, and we could grow it without thinking about it, just the colour He approved! It would save so much time and bother, to say nothing of expense. But as we cannot, we must be careful that there should be always, whether we are in uniform or not, on duty or off, that perfect harmony between the outward appearance and the inward possession.

Nothing could be worse, I think, than inconsistency in this. How we love the sweet consistency of nature. A violet is a violet, easily recognized as such, whether in bud or in full bloom. How disconcerting to find it to all appearances a poppy at one stage of its existence, and a dandelion at another! Yet I have met salvationists——!

This letter is already longer than you are likely to relish. I remember your aversion to anything that lasts too long, especially if it is in the nature of a lecture.

Does it matter greatly to you what you wear? Ought it to matter so much? Surely, it is the sort of thing one can gladly and easily renounce in case there should be in it an element of danger to any who might be influenced, or a tendency to lower the standard of separation from the world that has been set up.

Think it over, and be resolved that there shall ever be in you that sweet consistency in dress and manner, in word and deed, as shall mark you out as a child of the Most High—in the world, but not of it.

Yours, to serve

26
THAT SUPERANNUATED
SCRUBBING BRUSH AND TIMBREL

MAY 1916

My Dear G____,

I was reminded of you the other evening by a scrubbing brush and a tambourine—both ancient and both retired from active service. Not that I mean to imply that you are! Far from it. Still, I was reminded of you, and so I am writing.

Do you remember the two articles in question? They now decorate the wall of my room at the Lodge. The other day the brush had a narrow escape. Having fallen from his right place, he was picked up by an indignant cadet, who marched him off to the lower regions, grumbling over the carelessness of some one who had left a scrubber in the major's room! It was rescued, fortunately for me—and the cadet.

Certainly, it is not a thing of beauty, nor of use, yet it is dear to me. I do rather like a tangible reminder of the unseen, and the old thing represents much. I remember the day I sorted it out from among many brethren in the old bucket room. I was 'on the dining room' then, and we scrubbed it every day when I was a cadet. I'm afraid we were inordinately proud of the colour of the boards. This particular brush was selected because of two qualifications—it was light, having lost the top half of its wooden back; and its bristles were short and stiff. It did good service, being carefully hidden away after use; and when I left the Training College I took it with me, and have had it within view ever since.

Now, quite close to it hangs my Training College tambourine. Together they tell me many things from time to time—some things that I wish I could pass on to you just as they come to me; but, alas! mere words, especially on paper, do not speak as clearly as those two old dears!

For one thing, they call me so cheerily back to the past, not in a melancholy 'God-be-with-you-till-we-meet-again' style, but in a jolly 'Oh-good-old-way-how-sweet-thou-art' fashion. They remind me how really splendid it was to be a cadet, and to have enjoyed being one, and how still more wonderfully joyful to have had, and still to have, a chance of going ahead with the work.

When I look at the scrubber, the actual companion of

the first duties that entering the work entailed, I am glad it means to me now, as it meant then, the work of the hands as well as of the heart and mind. 'Body, soul, and spirit, Jesus, I give to Thee.'

If I were ever in danger of getting above scrubology, I hope the sight of the old original would make me ashamed. Just now I often wish there were more opportunity for that kind of service, but the wish is rather a lazy one. It has always been an easier thing to me to serve others in *doing* something for them than by merely talking to them, especially when they seldom really want to hear what you have to say. How strangely, truly grateful people seem for some service to the body, and how slow to value a service to the spirit; though the latter costs the giver beyond all comparison more than the former. If the practical had been hardest to me, probably the Lord would have given me that to do, for He knows there is ever the greatest blessing in the service that costs most.

However, whether I have many chances or few the old brush tells me to take them, to see to it that I live up to the old ideal of anything and everything as a love service to souls and bodies for Jesus' sake. It tells me also that it is the spirit that sanctifies the work, as it truly did when I scrubbed the dining room in those dear old Training College days. So now we can—I can—you can do all in the spirit of the Lord Jesus. Isn't it wonderful to realize it?

The tambourine joins in all the time, and particularly emphasizes that I must be cheerful and courageous. When I first used it I was a fearing, feeble creature. The tambourine often helped me to hide that fact, and perhaps I began to learn what it meant to offer the sacrifice of praise in those first days of playing—how to praise when it would have been easier to grumble! The cheerful sound of jingles is symbolical of that brave spirit that helps me to smile in the face of failure—anyway, in face of aggravations.

I wish I had a more naturally smiling face and a less worrying spirit; because I do believe in the 'Happy Sally' religion. That's one of the things that the tambourine stands for to me—so I still play one, as well as listen respectfully to what my pensioned one says.

We do need a bit more of the pluck that first made the tambourine a part of the armour of a Hallelujah lassie. It seems to me it was like cheeking the devil—shaking it in defiance of every preconceived notion—bringing it in to add to the joyful noise in the very heart of the devil's strongholds. So they played them down in the slum alleys and in the courts, making music of a special sort. You cannot play a tambourine without feeling, or at least showing a bold front to the foe. That's one reason why I wish we beat it more often.

Do you ever play one? Whether you do or not, I hope the spirit is still there—that sort of reckless, dare-the-devil confidence in God; so that

> When Satan's dart attacks my heart,
>   By faith I vanquish Hell;
> And go on singing through the storm—
>   'Tis with the righteous well.

Singing through the storm! God give us hearts brave enough to go on doing it; and surely, sometimes, if not always, the tambourine may help us. In some places the soldiers are too respectable to welcome them, but sinners still associate them with us, and the jingle of the tambourine has often announced the presence of the Army to a backslider.

This almost seems as though I were taking it for granted you never use one—further, that I am pleading its cause. I am doing neither. I am thinking much more of what was represented by the tambourine in early days, and we women of the Salvation Army must keep up the standard, and if incidentally that meant here and there a little more tambourine, well, I should like it.

Anyway, there they are on the wall, the brush and the timbrel—worn out, valueless; and one day they will land on the dust heap either by accident or design. But I do pray that, for me, while I live, the gospel of each may be part of my religion. To serve, and to serve with joy; not only inside joy, but joy expressed in such a fashion as others may know my work *is* a joy—courage to rejoice in hope even when I cannot in fact, and love to serve even in the lowest, with such a spirit as shall raise it to the highest.

It is ages since I heard from you, and longer still since I saw you; but I should like to see you, and feel sure that you would not feel awkward with either a scrubber or a tambourine—whichever circumstances demanded. I can truthfully say I should not.

> Yours, serving with joy

27
CONCERNING THE UNEXPECTED

My Dear B____,

The days do slip by, especially when they are as crowded as ours! I am finding it difficult to believe so many have already passed since I saw you.

The other day, before the end of the session, I came over from the Lodge feeling rather tired and flat. The night had not been exactly successful—they seldom are just before commissioning—and that particular morning I was under a sense of heaviness that made me shrink from, rather than welcome, the new day.

I went wandering into the office, my thoughts gathering reluctantly, to face the day's problems, when I noted a small but unexpected splash of colour on the desk. There, sitting in a little glass mug, was a small party of wild orchids. A bright, clear, purple patch, so fresh and sprightly, looking almost businesslike in their uprightness. There were only a few of them, and I am not sure now how they got there. I only know I did not expect them, and that finding them had an effect on me that helped me all through that day.

They were truly to me messengers of the Lord, meeting me in a way and at a time when I was not looking forward to anything so nice and cheering. Sometimes, I think, the message met in unexpected places has been the most precious of all, and so the other night when I was thinking of you, and imagining you in your new surroundings, I did pray that in unlooked-for ways the Lord might meet you, speaking to your heart that which it needs to hear.

I hope that you are fully believing that God *does* understand how much you are needing in so many ways. He truly does, and will meet your need; though perhaps not in the way you thought. Are you on the look-out for Him? If you are, you will not miss Him; though the manner of His coming may sometimes be as silent as the stealing in of a sunbeam, and clothed with such simplicity that, unless your faith's eye is keen, you might only see the 'ordinary thing' that your hands might handle.

Be watching, too, for chances of being His messenger to others. I do not know who put the orchids in the little mug on my table that morning, or whether that one had any idea the Lord would use them to do me any good, but I am glad that they came there!

You may not realize how much may come from your quite simple act or word, but God does. Do not expect Him to give you a revelation beforehand of all that will come out of it, but be quick to *do*.

It seems to me as if the unexpected gift brings a joy all its own, just as there is a greater pleasure in finding the wild flower, because you are never quite certain where it will be, than in gathering grander and gayer flowers from the garden where they wait for you in the expected places.

Seek more diligently for the chance of doing the good you were *not* expected to do. It is often difficult to tell how hungry are souls for the little token of thought or gratitude—even high official souls! Scatter wild flowers of service and kindness that will be a delight to the tired or discouraged—perhaps more than you know. Let them peep out in all sorts of unexpected corners in the quarters—love's little surprise services—not only to those who are loved, but, in the name of the One you love, serving even the unlovable and ungrateful.

Of course, there is the other side to the picture. This morning a message was brought me, quite unexpected and distinctly annoying; but even with the unexpected trial comes unexpected grace if we instantly turn to the Lord.

No doubt you have found a good many trials of this sort; the kind you had not prepared for here in the Training College. I never warned you of them in FO class or at the Home Lodge, or anywhere, nor did any one else; yet they are cropping up like briars across the path where you thought all would be clear.

As I write, there comes to me this thought: does not the trial we could not prepare ourselves for discover to ourselves and to others our true state? It seems to me it is a more real test than any anticipated difficulty could be. Perhaps, too, one could say it gives opportunity for revealing to others what is our real attitude. In this sense our behaviour under a comparatively small trial that takes us by surprise, may win for us the confidence of some one who, without such a revelation, would never have trusted us.

Do you think you have anything fresh to discover about yourself? Perhaps an unexpected perplexity may show you undreamed-of capacity in yourself. We are often in the dark about ourselves. If we could only believe a little more deeply that God is not! The unexpected trial is often, I believe, the call to greater things; and if, instead of being alarmed, we were more ready to respond, we should find the new demand had led us into an altogether different conception of our own strength and knowledge, as well as having given us another token of how much God can do.

I fear I am not succeeding in making very clear to you what I mean. I have only been able to write this letter in fragments. This is the seventh attempt to finish it since I began. You need not be surprised, therefore, that it is not very connected! But this is what I want you to understand: Be watching for the messages of God in your own heart. You cannot tell how they may come, or of what they may consist, but live in the spirit of readiness to commune with Him, so that He should never send you a message you fail to recognize because you were not expecting Him.

Also, be always looking for the chance to give the good things people were not counting on you to give. Of course, you will give what they have the right to expect as well; but scatter as generously as you know how, the kind words, the approving smile, the loving services, that will be as sweet a surprise to souls as my orchids were to me that 'blue' morning.

Do not be discouraged in the face of the unexpected trials. Only be sure you meet God there. He allows us to be taken by surprise often that we may have no alternative but to cast ourselves on Him; then it is we learn how much faith can bring to us and out of us!

Above all, believe that 'Nothing is by chance in our lives; if we trust Him, all is by love.' I am believing it, so I am often helped by things I am sure the devil meant should cause me to lose the Blessing.

I will close with this word. It might one day be an unexpected pleasure to find a letter from you telling me frankly how things are with you! Now I must be off to a job which I *am* expected to do.

Yours, expecting you to be good
and do well

28
OF AGRICULTURE—SPIRITUAL AND OTHERWISE

JULY 1916

My Dear O____,

How can I say what I want to say in a way that will come home freshly to your heart? If I say it straight out, you will only answer me as you did once when we were talking—'it's easy for you to *say*, Major'—implying, of course, that I know nothing of the difficulties that lie between saying and performing.

It is a difficult thing to make another understand how one's own soul has travelled the same path: chiefly, perhaps, because the things that make the real anguish of the way lie in one's own self, and not on the road one treads.

Shall I tell you a story? The days of your light-hearted youth—Training College days, of course, I mean—are not so far passed but that you can remember how glad you always were to find a story sandwiched between the 'summary' points. This story is not interesting, and it is not true; not even good from the standpoint of description, because the bounds of a letter, to say nothing of my time, forbid. But it has a moral.

Two brothers were given a portion of land for a fixed period. They were young, inexperienced, and independent. Each was anxious for a goodly result for labour bestowed. The one found his land, sloping gently towards the south, fertile soil, easy to manipulate with the simplest tools. The morning sun embraced it and the evening sun kissed it. It was well watered. Here, without great knowledge, one could hope to gather a rich harvest. He cast in his seed, and, rejoicing every day, watched the quick growth; tending here and there the springing life and resting at leisure when the sun was hot; dreaming sweet dreams in the cool evening, and putting in order the barns that were already built to receive the year's fruits.

The other looked with great longing at the beauty and richness of his brother's portion, turning heavy-hearted to his own barren patch. Here were no barns, and only stony ground. Cold winds that swept down from the hills nipped the tender shoots. The sun rose late over the crest, and, as though tired of his sidelong glance at so unpromising a prospect, hurried off the scene as early as might be. Then the shadows gathered quickly until they darkened into night.

What manner of harvest could be produced here? However, being young and independent, as well as somewhat ambitious, his was not the spirit to sink into idle hopelessness, still less into idle jealousy or complaint. He rose early and stayed awake late. He toiled at the earth till the muscles of his arms and back grew hard and tough. As he worked, his mind planned new tools that would enable him to deal more effectively with the special difficulties of his ground. He devised cunning screens of brushwood to break the force of the winds. After weeks of effort he constructed a sort of pump that made the distribution of water less arduous, and, with infinite labour, he built rough barns for storage.

But, in spite of unrelenting toil, as the seasons of harvest came round, he worked ever with a heavy heart, gathering handfuls where he felt his labour had measured sheaves. Sometimes he heard news of the rapidly increasing stores of his brother, and wondered that the Giver should have made gifts so widely differing in opportunity.

At last came the end of the time appointed, and the Giver went over the ground with each of the brothers. Results were hardly to be compared. The owner of the south land displayed, with joy, overflowing barns, richness in fruit and flower, and the Giver rejoiced with him. But to the brother whose barns were small and poorly filled, whose grain was scanty and fruits few (so few that they seemed hardly worth showing, and the bronzed face of their owner was clouded as in mind he compared the tangible results with what, during those long days of toil, he had hoped might be), he gave a message of great import.

Walking along one of the rough home-made paths with a hand on the young man's shoulder, the Giver told him of a great estate, land of almost limitless worth, largely undeveloped. After describing in few words the opportunity, he added that he had been searching for a man able to take charge of it, and he had decided that the one with whom he now walked should be he. 'But I have not succeeded,' he replied. 'Ought you not to choose my brother, whose harvests have been great, whose barns are full? He will have learned how to deal with the heavy crops that spring up in rich land.'

Then the Giver explained that in this he had been watching not only for filled barns and much fruit, but most of all for the development of the man who worked. 'The barren land you have tilled,' he said, 'has given you that which is more precious than well-filled barns and rich stores: an arm strong to work, an eye keen to see the possibilities of unlikely spots, a mind quick to devise new methods and means. Above all, you know how to value the fruit that costs so much to produce, and still to hope, and because of hope to work, when wind and weather join to make reaping days only as dreams.'

Sometimes the fruit produced in the farmer is of greater import than that produced on the farm! So it is also that this story may help to make clear to you why you are where you are.

Also—for you are still a child in some moments—you may be wanting to say to me: 'Why could not the story have been quite different? Why could not the brother of the fertile south lands have developed himself and sought out ingenious devices, and strengthened his muscles with hard work, and so had yet greater harvests and been honoured in the end with the greater opportunity?'

Yes, why not? To answer you fully would take more time than I have at my disposal now, and when I had finished you might only wonder what I was driving at! I only add this, therefore: Brothers or sisters—we human creatures seldom exert ourselves unduly, unless necessity be laid upon us. If we can succeed—find what we need or want—without great efforts or sacrifice, why make it? The fact is, we are mostly blind to the result of effort and sacrifice *in* us, and are generally thinking only of results outside ourselves.

God, who is perfecting that which concerns *us*, as well as working for others through us, often thrusts us into circumstances that will as nearly as possible compel certain activities on our part; not only because of some results that may accrue for the enriching of the Heavenly Kingdom on earth in the hearts and lives of others, but chiefly because of the effect on our own spirit and character.

One day, perhaps sooner than we know—its nearness probably depends on how we tackle the stony patch we are now working at—He, the Giver, wants to trust us with wide lands of opportunity. We must be strong and skilled. Strong with the strength that springs from strenuous labour; skilled with skill that is given only to actual experience.

And so, before I close, I quote Paul: 'Beloved, let us not be weary in well-doing; for in due season we shall reap, if we faint not.'

Believe it about the harvest of handfuls that you are going to bring in rejoicing from the highways and byways of X____; but most of all, believe it about the harvest in *you*, over which the Lord Himself shall rejoice—that harvest of a tender love, a more steadfast faith, a more enduring patience, a more determined purpose—a character with well-developed powers—a heart that has learned the lesson of hope, because it dwelt in a land where there were many days in which, if there had not been a 'rejoicing in hope', there had been no rejoicing at all. And every one knows that to do good work you must find joy in it somehow, even if there are sometimes tears too.

Are you like the brother with the barren patch? Well, may the end of my story come true for you. But until then, 'let patience have her perfect work, that ye may be perfect' when the time comes!

God's Presence be with thee ever.

29

THE GRACE OF APPRECIATION

SEPTEMBER 1916

My Dear D____,

How mysterious life is! Even in those phases of it with which we are most familiar. Sometimes I feel that all our knowledge is a merely superficial contact with matters we 'know not of'. What makes my eye a seeing eye? What is sound? Are you a little imaginative? Do your thoughts go leaping the boundaries of time and space until they are brought to sudden standstill by the most mysterious question of any perhaps: why and how you came to be *you*?

Have you ever awakened in the early morning to find that 'why' perched upon your pillow, impudently insistent, for you have not been able to answer it before. What *are* you? What has been in the past? What is in the future? How is it that you find yourself in the 'now' of the universe? Why is life thrust upon you at all? And then have you noticed how differently you face the great fact that, in spite of questions and wonderings, you *are* a part of the living whole, and must up and do in your day.

Sometimes there stirs in you a spirit that magnifies every sense of strength of which you are conscious. The actual burdens and sorrows of life's little day are only as the dust under your feet. Your spirit rises to another atmosphere. Faith joins you to the infinite powers of an Everlasting God. You are not of the dust returning to dust, but of the immortal looking for a new heaven and a new earth; and finding, in the dear earth of the present, daily opportunity for triumphing over every degrading and selfish impulse. Consciously strong, you step forth almost eagerly: no sin shall soil your soul, no sorrow break your spirit, no hope deferred make your heart sick. You triumph in temptation, and rejoice in sacrifice, with a joy that cannot be explained.

> Raised by the breath of Love Divine,
> You urge your way with strength renewed.

The 'why' is not answered, but you are glad to 'be', and to have the chance of helping some other soul out of the dust of time into the fresh air of eternity—for does not faith make today just a part of the 'for ever'?

Then, alas! there are those days when no such sense of

inherent strength moves in you. The thought of the greatness of the creation seems to suffocate the feeble pulse of life. How shall *you*—small, weak, inconstant atom—cope with forces that you but dimly perceive, yet that surround and impel you? Have there not been, God knows! past efforts, and as truly past defeats? How brace yourself to the conflict of another day or even another hour?

At such a moment how much may depend upon the influence of some one or something outside ourselves? How easily the smoking flax may be quenched, the bruised reed broken? On the contrary, how miraculously many a soul has stepped out towards the steep that led to victory because some voice whispered, 'You ought to win, you *can win*.'

I believe, when I began to write this, I was going to say something about the mystery of intruding thoughts. What controls our thoughts? I know, in a general sense, the character of a man's thoughts will be largely decided by what they have been; that is, by what is already gathered in the man's experience, so that the same occurrence may start into being quite a different train of thought in two minds. But what decides the actual thought when so many others might as reasonably have been presented? We may expel a thought the instant we recognize it as unworthy (I hope you are becoming an expert at this), remembering always 'as a man thinketh in his heart, so is he.' The presentation of thought to the mind is one of the mysteries that interests me.

The other day I was in a garden, weeding, in fact, and in a world of thought into which the smell of earth and green things often leads me for rest and refreshment. In the garden next door children came to play, and every few moments after their appearance, there spread over the wall to me the sound of voices varying in volume and distinctness according to the age of the owner, but always sweet as well as eager, crying, 'Look, Mummie, look!' '*Now* look, Mummie!'

I did not hear any response, but from the pause ensuing, followed, after an interval, by the happy repetition of the cry, I easily concluded that from some shady nook 'Mummie' lifted her loving eyes and smiled her approval as often as it was sought. Now, why should that make me think of you? I can trace no link. I tried to at the time, but failed. The weeding went on, but my thoughts were with you and your problems.

Still the children in the garden trilled out the same phrases, and still the play went merrily, and still I thought of you, moralizing a little to myself at the same time with the babies' words for text.

Do you think your grown-up children, who just now

are not very happy together in life's game, could be made happier, taught to play better, if your approval were easier to gain? Is there not in us all an active, healthy desire for approbation? Like all other appetites, if over-indulged it becomes a tyrant and quite hateful; but it is there as a part of us, and I believe could be used to help people.

Here is brother Scratchy, so apt in finding fault with others, so contrary in make-up, that it seems instinct with him to want the opposite to your wish, immediately he knows it. If, somehow, you could find some point about him or his doings with regard to which you could honestly say, 'How well done! How wise of you!' he would be helped to feel you appreciative. His love of approbation would probably urge him to try to please you again, and from the moment he begins really to want your approval, if you are tactful, you begin to be able to deal with his faults.

Poor Sergeant W___, hard-worked man that he is, with his muddley little home and sickly wife. How often he must struggle through the day, feeling it to be *not* worth living, depressed, and, as a result, sometimes sour, if not bitter! How much do you think a word of praise from the captain would mean? How far could the feeling that you were noticing and expecting, spur him to some new effort that would lift him above his dingy circumstances and help to make a new man of him?

'England expects every man to do his duty.' How many thousands have been stimulated to do their duty by these words since they were first uttered by a man who knew how to lead men? To me the secret of their inspiration lies in the word 'expects'.

England—Nelson—the captain—some one expects *me* to do my duty; and because of that expectation I must not fail, but, like the children playing in the garden, be able to cry to the expecting one, 'Look at me—I win!'

The miracle is that in someone's heart and mind there should have sprung up an expectation about himself greater than W___'s own, and rather than forfeit that someone's approval he is spurred to make the effort that changes him.

Perhaps in all kinds of dumb and unbeautiful ways many have cried, and some still cry, for that smile of recognition that should bring them new inspiration. But, no; the captain was too busy seeing faults that badly needed correcting, and so the approving look was not given; and who knows how many have sunk silently down defeated?

Revive them by some beautiful expectation about them that you make known to them; and watch, and let them find you watching, even if some disappoint you;

and, though you find your eyes must smile their praise to one through the mist of tears shed for another, do not withhold the smile. The captain in the corps should be like the mother in the garden, approving every good effort, encouraging all—but especially the young—by judicious praise, and inspiring each with the knowledge of individual expectancies of them. *God gives you the position that makes your approval a thing sought for.* See that you use it so as to strengthen the weak, lead the unruly, and hasten the coming of the Kingdom of the Lord.

You are doing well, from what I hear; so I close this letter smiling my approval on you, and still expecting greater things.

30
TO THE SERGEANTS AND CADETS OF ___ SESSION

My Dear Girls,

I have wanted so much to write you—the whole crowd of you! The new cadets are here, and every now and then I am reminded of someone who *was* a new cadet once on a time, but who *now* is a lieutenant or captain somewhere or other.

Do you know, I wonder, how badly I want to see you all? I fancy it would be an all-night sitting if we could meet together in the lecture hall, with time to hear everybody's testimony, and make sure—looking at some of you would be enough to tell me—that all is well with you in that which concerns the spiritual life. How good, how very good, it would be! As it is I am missing you in a way that makes me almost *not* want the 'new ones'.

Everything goes on much as usual. Colonel read the rules and chaffed the girls, and we laughed much, as we did when you were here, but had much of importance to ponder over as well, just as you did; and by now all are beginning to look real cadets. Do *you* still look so? I mean, if you were all together in the old place again, would you look as though you matched it, or should I want to put you in order (do your hair, or tie your bonnet strings) before Colonel saw you? I like to think that you would not be changed, but be really looking what I hope you are—sincere, unworldly, Salvation soldiers.

The first set of 'lodgers', travel daily to and fro, and the tramp of the feet past the office window has begun again. The sergeants sang together in the meeting tonight. It was very nice; but *I* heard other sergeants singing, and I shall not go to the sergeants' room tonight to hurry them off to bed. I should see too many ghosts there.

Dear girls, all of you. You do still belong to the old place, whether you deserve to or not! You know you do, and many, very many of you, are going to be a credit to it in the highest sense. I do not really want you back. As I often told you, you only came in to go out, and God is able to use your present surroundings to help you, as truly as He used these Training College days, if you are in touch with Himself.

Do not let anybody be discouraged. Do not let anyone

give up. Do not let any of you settle down to be anything less than you resolved to be by the Lord's help when you were here. I expect some of you are finding progress slower than you thought it would be; perhaps, because you do not realize that God is working in you with regard to things that you have not considered much. He does not always bring to quick perfection in us those fruits of the Spirit we are coveting in particular. He may see that it is better that our patience should be perfected before our courage, or our humility before our zeal. So long as we *are* growing, we must not be disheartened that there is still so much to reach.

All the roses on the rose bush do not bloom at the same hour. Do not be depressed because some spiritual quality in you is only a bud, when you see the perfect fruit in another. Thank the Lord there is the bud, and let prayer and faith and effort go on. There will be flower and fruit of that particular kind in you one day.

On the other hand, because you do not see in someone else the spiritual quality you had counted on, do not judge them or be disappointed. That soul may be rich in a fruit of which your soul has little perception. The orange tree would be a good illustration of spiritual life. On the same tree, I believe, at the same time, may be found all the stages from flower to ripe fruit. You must learn to distinguish between imperfect development and barrenness. All must be fruit-bearers, but all our fruit will not be perfect at once.

The General is coming for a Spiritual day. The 'new ones' will hardly be able to value it fully; you would, now that for you there can, in the same sense, be no more such. But if there is alive in you the same spirit of seeking and desire, God will come as truly to meet *you* as He will to meet the new cadets.

Is there the same spirit in you? New battles, new temptations, new everything; but the earnest, sincere, believing heart will find God near. Nothing need separate you from God, and His Presence means every soul-need supplied and every soul-quality strengthened.

Yes, that gives me hope for you all—the Lord's nearness to each; unless you have set up a barrier. If any of you have done this, break it quickly down, and come back to the place of the child in spirit before God.

Perhaps, now you are gone, it is even easier for me to see you fulfilling the ideal—really being what I felt it was in you to be, than it was when you were here. All of you held such possibilities, surprises for the devil and the doubters.

I think of many of you, one by one, and see you gaining strength where you were weak; love, faith, humility, beautifully interpreted by your every day's service and sacrifice. You *are* walking with the Lord Jesus 'all the way from earth to Heaven'. Have I the right so to think of you? I mean *is* it so?

'O Lord Jesus, I pray Thee, let it be so. May each one walk with Thee, and wilt Thou perfect Thy work in every heart. Fulfil all Thy high purposes. Teach them, O God, to count on Thy present help, so that believing, none may shrink from Thy commands or shirk Thy cross. May all—yes, Lord, *all*—come in the end to that perfect image of Thyself, which is Thy will for every soul. Amen.'

31
TO ONE WORKING
UNDER A SENSE OF INJUSTICE

NOVEMBER 1916

My Dear B____,

Since our conversation together the other day, I have thought a good deal over what you said. I hope you did not feel I was making light of the situation from your standpoint. I know that to be faced with the necessity of working under a sense of injustice is one of the most trying experiences.

Humanly speaking, it does at present appear as though your past effort had not been valued, and that you are likely to have to fight again very much alone, and very little appreciated. Do let the fact that you succeeded in your last appointment be a strength to you now. It is the devil's trick to twist things so that you are tempted to feel it would be easier to accept the present, if you had failed in the past! Don't you see that as things now are, you do not need to reproach yourself, but can the more confidently commit the whole set of circumstances to God?

It does not help matters that the innocent man should wish he had been guilty, in order that he might deserve the punishment that has fallen upon him. Had you failed, you might have had the poor comfort of knowing you deserved the present hardness; but, surely, the thought of the past victory can come to you now as an assurance of victory to be won?

I am anxious that this experience should do you good and not harm. It might do either; and it is in the hope of helping you to gain, and not lose by it, that I write.

You do realize that this is an experience likely to be repeated? If, therefore, it has power to rob you of your joy and confidence, it will be a powerful weapon in the hand of the enemy; and in the end you might even be driven from the field altogether, having no heart for the fight.

Review the position for a moment. Are you to expect to be as much affected by external things as you would be if you were without religion? If not—and we do agree there, I know—what is to make the difference? It is not that we suffer less under a sense of injustice. I think we sometimes suffer more. At least, it is often harder to suffer in the right spirit than if one might blaze forth in righteous anger toward the instrument of injustice. It is not that we find no pleasure in human approbation or reward. We do. It is not that it has ceased to matter to us whether we make progress in our work or not. Ambition for God can be as strong as a selfish ambition, and therefore as open to disappointment. In all these and similar matters we are likely to *feel* as keenly as the man without religion.

Is there, then, anything in religion that can make a practical difference to us at these times? If not, much that we say about the comfort and joy of it must be humbug! Unless we have help at the point where the human fails, we might almost as well be without. Were we less inclined to seek it outside ourselves, we should find there *is* that in our experience that can make all the difference. Think a moment, and you will know what I mean—*the assurance of God's favour*. We are so constantly engaged in pressing this home on others, that sometimes, I am afraid, we are not as careful as we should be to maintain the experience. It seems to me that next to faith in God, this *is* the secret of strength and joy and comfort. It was for Job: 'All the while my breath is in me, and the spirit of God is in my nostrils, my lips shall not speak wickedness, nor my tongue utter deceit. God forbid that I should justify you: till I die I will not remove mine integrity from me. My righteousness I hold fast, and will not let it go. My heart shall not reproach me so long as I live.' It was for David, for the martyrs, and today for you and for me. No one can rob us of it, if it is ours. Without it, there is no soul-satisfying set of circumstances. With it, any are bearable.

X____ wrote me a letter a day or two ago that was a blessing to me. In it she said, 'But, Major, it comes with a great peace to my soul when I realize that the Blood of Jesus has cleansed me from all sin, and that He has made it impossible for me to tolerate anything which is not strictly true and honourable, and just and pure, and I love the Lord for giving me this experience.'

Yes, and the joy of it will be her strength in many a dark day.

Have you really kept it? Is the secret of your courage and hope rooted in that inward knowledge of rightness before God? It gives confidence in prayer, and adds hope to faith, because it brings a sense of having the *right* to count on God.

I have just been taking prayers with the sergeants, and we read the words of the Lord: 'Watch ye therefore and pray always, that ye may be accounted worthy . . . to stand before the Son of man.' And we sang:

> Make me like Thyself below,
>   Unblamable in grace.
> Ready, prepared, and fitted here
> By perfect holiness to appear
>   Before Thy glorious face.

If we could only realize more that we *are* in His Presence already! The joy comes when we know that, and are not ashamed.

For you just now, it seems to me that this assurance of acceptance in His sight is like a strong arm of comfort for your discouraged spirit to lean upon. Even your own feelings of disappointment and anxiety for the future do not affect the realness of the experience, if it is yours. Whose condemnation really matters? You may be hurt for the moment, but before God you are justified; and, in the sunshine of His smile, the shadow of man's prejudice or blame ceases to count.

Pray that this present difficulty may help you to live more truly that life of mutual agreement—you and the Lord in full accord about *all* you undertake—and you will be less dependent upon people's opinions; and, what is more important still, there will spring up a greater confidence in God's power to overrule for you. When you are certain about *your* attitude toward *Him*, it is easier to believe that all is working for good toward *you*. You may have a difficult time in your present appointment; it may be that you will never, humanly speaking, feel it acceptable to you; but it may be wonderfully the place of triumph for your soul.

> Whate'er pursuits my time employ,
>   One thought shall fill my soul with joy:
> That silent, secret thought shall be
>   That all my hopes are fixed on Thee.
> On Thee, my Lord, on Thee.

This is our secret—yours. Neither man nor devil can rob us of the joy of it; and often when humanly we should be utterly crushed, the crushing outward circumstances only make our secret joy more noticeably precious. Instead of being cast down, or bitter, or slack and unenthusiastic in the face of adverse circumstances, we can say with X____, 'I love the Lord for giving me this experience.' The joy of it will make you able to bear the burden of actualities in the shape of unappreciative superior officers, discouraging appointments, and the continued loneliness of uncongenial companionships. But it all comes back to the question of possessing the Lord's full favour in everything.

Yet *now* I know Thee as the hidden Bread,
    The Living One who died,
Who sitteth at my table, by my bed,
    Who walketh at my side.

I pass within the Glory even now,
    Where shapes and words are not;
For joy that passeth words, O Lord, art Thou,
    A bliss that passeth thought.

I enter there, for Thou hast borne away
    The burden of my sin;
With conscience clear as Heaven's unclouded day,
    Thy courts I enter in.

Heaven now for me—for ever Christ and Heaven—
    The endless now begun—
No *promise*—but a gift eternal *given*,
    Because the work is done.

    Yes. Hallelujah!

32
THE YOUNG AND RESOURCEFUL

DECEMBER 1916

My Dear T____,

Did you notice on the front page of a recent 'War Cry' an article which drew attention to the work of 'young and resourceful officers'? Of course, I read it at once, because I knew it must be about one or other of our girls. Any good thing spoken of you is a joy to me always.

'Young and resourceful!' The first is true enough of you! As to the second, in a measure it has yet to be proved. The dictionary describes 'resource' as 'a new source; any source of aid; contrivance; device.' Resourceful, therefore, applied to the Salvation Army officer, must mean a new source, contrivance, device, for soul-saving.

I do hope you deserve the title! I have thought a good deal of you, especially since I saw you; and I must say it has been a little disappointing to me that you have not succeeded better in getting hold of sinners.

In class the other day, I was asking the cadets to give me their thought as to the reason the Army ribbon was so seldom used for converts. One girl thought that in some cases the officers did not trouble because they found their predecessors had not. I am not sure that it was a very convincing statement, but I do wonder if in things more important you have been content with what *has* been, as a measure of what *can* be.

You told me that the corps has always been hard for soul-saving. Was I mistaken, or did you say it in a way which indicated that you had *accepted the fact as inevitable?* Your predecessors found it so, and—so do you. But—*you* are young and resourceful! Youth and resource combined should, surely, mean the doing of something not before attempted; and by God's blessing, the result might be something better than before experienced.

I do not think I need reassure you by making my pen write it down on paper, that I *do* believe in and hope for and love you; you are one of the young officers; and it goes without saying that I do. I do not mean, of course, that many of the old officers are not better and braver than you are; but I have not known them, and prayed over them as I have over you, and that makes just all the difference. I respect and honour them for what they are and for their past victories; but for you and many others I feel a personal sense of longing expectation, born of your training days. I should like to feel that all of you deserved the title 'resourceful'. I should like to be sure that *you* do.

What a multitude of things the old officers must have *done for the first time* in the hope of getting hold of some sinner! If one way failed, they tried another. Are *you* going to be behind?

Colonel Jeffries was here on business some time ago, and speaking to me said: 'On the whole, the young officers are doing well. They are good and sincere and hard working, but I've noticed that where they do fairly well in keeping the corps together and helping the young people, they certainly do not succeed in getting big sinners saved so well as many of the older FOs.'

I have thought a good deal over the Colonel's words. He is a person whose opinion I think worth having. I have prayed, too, that God might show me if we could do any better here in the Training College. I wonder if we could have done better with you?

My dear T____, what is the use of being young and resourceful, if you are not succeeding in getting hold of big sinners? *That* is why God made the Salvation Army—to win 'souls, and the worst'.

I am awfully afraid the Colonel would consider you an illustration of his remark to me. You are sincere and good—I know that. You *do* work. You are keeping your corps together. You are helping your young people, but you have had few fresh cases of conversion. Yet there are plenty of sinners—big ones—in your district.

Why is it? I know you are very busy; that you have to face an increasing amount of corps business—the forms you must fill in are almost as many as the stars in heaven! I know the soldiers are exacting and unsatisfactory, and claim much time. Still, I do not see that any of these demands, or all of them, justifies the case. Even if they do, you would be right in neglecting some of them in order to go after souls; for the great fact remains that, unless we are saving sinners, our very existence as an Army is not justified. A Salvation Army that does not save!

I do sympathize with you in the rush—meetings every night but one, and inefficient 'locals'; yet there ought to, and *must*, be a way of combining soul-saving and corps organizing.

Have you realized that sinners nearly always need finding and seeking individually, one by one? Ninety-nine in the fold, the shepherd goes to seek that *one* which was lost. Have you made the mistake of thinking that the ninety-nine were more important, and the *one* not worth while?

Would you try going for one—say this next month— one really big out-and-out sinner? Somehow, I think you could do a good deal without robbing any other duty to an appreciable extent. Being young and resourceful, you will think of many things that could be done. I suggest one or two.

Settle who it shall be. Tell the corps, and ask all the soldiers to pray. If you do not think it wise to give the name, say something which will make the individual a reality to the corps. Call him your 'special case'. But why not give the name? If a man is well known for his sin, it's no disgrace to be prayed for. Visit his home regularly, and seek to do some practical service for wife or child. Find out what 'pub' he frequents, and talk to him there. Without letting him know it is arranged, plan to meet him on his way home from work, and have a word. Supply him with a paper. Live up to the dictionary definition. Find by prayer and with love's quick sight, 'a new source; any source of aid; contrivance; device', to win his soul.

It occurs to me as I write that Christmas is coming! What could I wish better for you than that the Spirit of Christ should so possess you as to work again through you for the saving of His lost?

You are young—may you see many Christmas days, and may each find you more resourceful than the last in all that has to do with helping and saving souls! For this, in you and in many others, I 'keep on believing'.

33

THOSE OLD LOCALS

JANUARY 1917

My Dear A____,

Do you think of field drill class sometimes? And thinking of it, do you remember your attempt at a word-picture? I do! I wonder if you have improved on that line? Whether or not, just for the sake of those old associations, here is a word-picture for your criticism.

'He wears a long-service badge, on a not too new uniform. His cap has seen better days, having been exposed to all weathers for some time. From under the peak of it look out two kindly eyes. The rather hard, strong face is softened by an iron grey beard. The hands are hard with work, and when holding a pen, are not as quick as yours or mine. His shoulders are bent, and give the whole man an aspect creating the impression that life has been heavy to bear. He is, or was, or will be, your treasurer!'

My word-picture does not allow me to speak of what I cannot see, so I leave it, and tell you he was giving his first testimony in the open-air when you were lying in your mother's arms. All the years *you* played and went to school and grew from childhood to womanhood, *he* marched in the little procession to the Army Hall. Several times in every week he asked for the collection, and often went round for it with his cap. Each Friday since the days when your total income amounted to one penny per week, he has toiled through the process known as 'making up the books', counting money that was not his, begging for it, planning to spend it, making up 'even money' from his hard-earned store.

He comes now to the open-airs and meetings with a regularity that would be astounding if it were not taken for granted from its very certainty.

Do you think he has been doing this all these years without having arrived at the conclusion that he knows a little about the best way of dealing with the corps? *You* would reckon to know when you had been at it as many weeks! Of course, he knows! He knows also a little about the ways of officers. He has seen better captains than you are. He has observed as many new attempts on the part of COs as you have celebrated birthdays.

When officers have succeeded and the corps has

flourished, he has worked on with little thanks or credit; and when officers have failed and all has been down and depressing, he has not only faced it, as far as the corps went, but often has borne the grumbles of the CO as well. He works for love of the concern, and every one seems to expect him to go on doing it.

His way of doing things is not up to date, perhaps; though in intention it is faithful. When he throws cold water over your proposals, it is because he truly thinks he is doing the best for the interests of the corps. His mind does not welcome innovations; but that is hardly his fault.

The treasurer of my imagining may stand as a type of a whole host of men and women 'locals'—warriors in the highest sense, perhaps in a higher sense than we shall ever be. They have fought on without the help of new surroundings, in the face of all kinds of difficulties, with very little gratitude, and seeing, in many cases, only small results for hours of toil. Now, in old age, instead of sitting beside the fire in comfort, taking it easy, the weather-beaten, warm-hearted old warriors are still 'going strong'.

But back to my old treasurer! I have described him to you as he is, and now *you* come on the scenes! You are young. 'The thoughts of youth are long, long thoughts'; do you expect this old man to travel with you at your speed? If he remonstrates, assures you that the plan was tried by Captain X____, and was not a success—advises you to wait until after 'SD'—shall you feel he is an old 'stick-in-the-mud', and wish he would send in his commission? The humdrum, as-it-was-in-the-beginning style, in which he asks for the collection tries you; but shall you be quick to forget how long he has been lifting up his voice on your behalf or on the behalf of others in the place you occupy?

What will be your attitude? Are you, with your superior education, your quick young mind, and strong young body, going to be 'bossy' and impatient? Shall your first resolve be to 'let the old chap know I'm the captain of this show'? Shall you *silently take it for granted* that the sergeant-major comes to the open-airs, and the secretary fills in the reports, and the YPS-M slogs with the children, and *only speak of what they don't do*? Shall you ask much of them, and not stop to consider whether you are giving what they might reasonably expect of you? Shall you judge their faults with quick, unerring accuracy, and belittle the services rendered? Shall the grey head and work-honoured hands supply you with incidents to smile at or complain about?

Or will you 'esteem them very highly in love for their work's sake', and love and serve them for their own sake, and let youth be careful to give reverence to age and experience? I do not mean give up all your plans because the 'locals' will not agree to them. I do not mean be governed by one or all of them. But I do mean win them by your humility in considering them, by honouring them, by going out of your way to bring to the notice of the corps their devoted toil by thanking them from your heart for their services, by avoiding in manner and speech, in their presence or out of it, anything that might look as though you had forgotten for the moment that somewhere you have a father and a mother for whom you would claim a different attitude on the part of one in your place.

To me, your command of the corps makes possible a picture of another sort. I see these old warriors of ours led forth by you, the contrast of your ages showing you and them to advantage, when the grace and joy of youth run to serve the gravity and wisdom of age. The cheeriness of your hope shines on them like the sun in winter. The zeal with which you expound your plans warms them to enthusiasm in spite of themselves. Your patience and tact smooth down the ruffles and allay the worries. Presently, because you have cared for them and honoured them, they begin to feel and care for you. Their eyes follow you as a father's, and you get advice as good as your mother's (or mine), as to not working too hard, etc.! A confidence is established that even their oddities cannot spoil, and from this centre flows a sense of unity and thoughtfulness for others that influences the whole corps.

So I think it could be. The 'locals' are, I know, not all such old dears as my treasurer. Some are young and more aggressive, but in the main these possibilities lie within each. The 'locals', no doubt, owe the officers of the Army much, but the officers also owe the 'locals' much. As far as you are concerned, I might, I think, lay down the law as to your attitude toward them, for they have all the right to expect from you at least the following consideration:

1. *The respect due to their office*—Have you learned to respect the place a man fills, apart from the man himself?

2. *A desire to have their opinion on all corps matters*—You will not necessarily follow it.

3. *A definite effort to help them spiritually*—Thus showing you recognize that their place in the corps demands a better experience than is expected of the soldier.

4. *An interest in their personal concerns*—As keen as you would like their interest in the corps to be.

5. *A delight in honouring them before their comrades and townsfolk*

6. *A faithfulness in dealing with them face to face about their faults*

7. *An occasional expression of thanks for even their everyday services*

It ought not to be possible for any 'local' to say, as I heard of a bandmaster saying the other day on being thanked for his Sunday's help: 'I've been a bandmaster twenty years, and this is the first time an officer of the corps has thanked me.'

It is a glory amongst us that our youth may lead, but you must so act toward the elders under your direction that your youth may never be your shame. 'Let no man despise thy youth, but be thou an example of the believers.'

Has it not been written: 'A little child shall lead them'? And why not, if that child's heart be filled with the love of God?

May your heart be so filled and kept filled, I pray, and, praying, believe.

34

IN TOUCH WITH SINNERS

MARCH 1917

My Dear C＿＿,

You would have revelled in the opportunity we had recently at Silvertown.* I do wish you could have been there. For one thing, you would have been pleased with the cadets. It did them a world of good, and many of them thoroughly forgot themselves. Anything which helps us to do that is a blessing. I truly believe nothing could have daunted some of them whilst they saw a chance of helping the people. What would it not be worth to them and the Army if they could always be so carried out of themselves!

I want to tell you a little of what I felt, because I want your opinion. You have been in the field some time now, and are in touch with a number of officers, some of longer, some of shorter experience than yourself; and you have had an opportunity not only of thinking things out, but also of judging from your own experience as well as from that of others, how far your 'thinkings' may be applied to the work.

Many things about our experiences on the scene of the disaster will never be forgotten. Danger, and death, and desolation, were seen in some of their most hideous forms, I suppose. No one could look on it all and not be stirred. Who could forget the flaming sky throwing into dark relief the ruined homes on all sides, the dumb despair of the people, the crushed and scorched bodies lying in the mortuaries.

All this, and enough to fill a book if I began to tell you of the people's individual courage, or of the multitude who, because of special need, claimed special interest and sympathy. But all those things fade in my mind before the one overwhelming revelation that those circumstances disclosed to me, of the actual daily life of the people; so that the circumstances themselves seemed only like a strikingly coloured curtain hung before a picture which, having seen, one remembers for ever.

We talked to them; we fished out their goods from the

* The scene of a disastrous explosion. Officers and cadets from the Training College, rallying at once to the spot, did splendid service amongst the distressed and injured people.

wreckage, and all the time we were seeing into the conditions of their lives, the darkness of their minds, the sordid miseries of their sins. Of their courage and thought for each other I could not say anything too good. Such people are worth saving from their wretched surroundings; from themselves; above all, from their sins.

And ever since those days spent amongst streets of small houses, so like other streets of small houses in other districts—ever since those days, C____, I have been asking myself: 'What is the Army doing for those people and their like? Are we fulfilling the expectations of our General, of those officers who, in the first days, fought for the liberty to work that we now enjoy? Are we doing what the people themselves expect of us? And, if not, why not?'

I was compelled to admit to myself that, but for the disaster that overtook them, the majority of those families would hardly have come in touch with a salvationist. Yet they are our sort of sinners.

Are you in touch with them in your district? Surely, no such disaster should be necessary to discover to us, as this one did, the old man of seventy odd who lived alone with his two cats, positively without a soul to care whether he was dead or alive. We found him sitting before the fire; one wall fallen in, windows out, and wreckage all around. How he escaped with his life was a miracle. He was the last to leave that street, and sat in the midst of his ruined home three days and nights after the other people had left, a helpless heap of human misery. Poor old dear! But think if the Army could have found him *before*, and made him understand there still was someone in the world to care, to whom he might send when the last enemy—death, drew near! To some of the forsaken 'old', life is surely more lonely, more cold, and more cruel than the grave.

The woman who loved the man who was not her husband, and who wished she were dead as well as he. The young wife—married at eighteen—living with her five children in two small rooms, who, looking at her husband's photo, on her return from the inquest where she gave evidence of identification, was heard to say half to herself: 'Yes, since Christmas, he was kinder.' The sergeant who was there said she felt afraid to ask what the woman meant. She had a pretty, girlish face, and bonnie children, the newly-made widow, but perhaps life will be easier without him than with him whose presence should have been the crowning joy of her home. What if the Army had found *him*, and turned him from the pub, and shown him the way to God, and so saved his manhood!

The circumstances of Silvertown are not exceptional. Any working-class population represents the same kind of need. *What are we doing to meet it?* The Army was raised up for these masses who are without God. Is it time we invented some new device, or have we given up using the old ones? How is it that our meetings go on, and we pray and preach often only to twenties and thirties, while the people perish by the thousand—broken, enslaved, degraded by their sin?

Are we making the mistake of occupying ourselves chiefly with the care of our corps instead of training our soldiers as fighters for souls? Are we so taken up making records of our work that there is hardly any time left for the work itself? Are we in our hearts believing that the devil's power is so great that we dare not challenge him? *Are we simply forgetting how the people live, because we so seldom go to see?*

Now, do write and tell me, for we are faced with the fact that in many corps there are very few sinners in the Sunday night meeting; but it is not because sinners are scarce.

It was just this state of things in the churches and chapels that drove our dear first General out to Mile End Waste—out to the sinners. In some of us who are content with our handful, or at least, who accept the few as inevitable, should there not be more of this driving power?

If the conditions of our work make it impossible to fulfil our duty to the sinner and to the Army, I believe we ought to find a plan which would change our conditions of work.

You are in the thick of it all. Tell me what is your experience. Is the FO out of touch with the mass of sinners among whom he lives? And if he is, whose fault is it?

I want to do better with the cadets. Now we say the purpose of an officer's life is to win souls, and that to fail in this is to fail in all. Ought we to be teaching them on different lines? In one thing I know you are with me, in feeling that, at all cost, we *must* be among the sinful. God called us for this, and made us an Army for this. And it is because I know you feel that, that I write you all this. You will understand how it weighs on my heart—this fear that in some places we are not doing what we exist to do.

God be with you.

Yours, as of old

35

SPRINGTIME IN THE SOUL

APRIL – MAY 1917

My Dear G____,

The family of violets arrived freshly sweet in their cool nest of moss. Your fingers know how to tuck the flowers in for a safe journey. They are still in the moss, but with their faces peeping out rather bashfully, making a contrast to the bold, self-important aspect of the ugly telephone beside them.

As I looked at them this afternoon they led my thoughts to the lines:

When the spring winds blow over the pleasant places,
The same fair things lift up the same fair faces.
    The violet is here!
It all comes back—the odour, grace, and hue;
Each sweet relation of its life repeated.
No blank is left, no longing for is cheated.
    It is the thing we knew.

Thank you for sending me messengers so sweet to tell me spring winds are blowing.

Is there spring in your soul, or do you find the trend of outward things producing the feeling of autumn—a sense that it is hard to hold on to what we have, let alone to be reaching out in expectancy of more; and a tendency to shiver at the prospect of a winter of darker days and fiercer storms ahead?

Several letters that have reached me lately show, between the lines, something of this apprehension, and I wonder about you. I should like to feel sure it is springtime with you. This has to do with our attitude toward God, as spring for the violet has to do with the earth's attitude toward the sun. For the heart turned resolutely toward Him there is the path shining more and more.

Do you really believe that in the world of your spirit it can be so? A perpetual spring, as in the lands of perpetual sunshine, where the new leaves replace the old without a break, and bare branches are never seen.

Have you ever visited the extreme north lands, where the sunny days of spring are few and the dark days of winter many? The earth, released only for a little spell from the iron grip of cold, thrusts up dwarfed trees and scanty herbage. The soil may be good, but before there is time to grow any fruitful thing the shadows creep back, and with them the frosts and snows, and all is dead until the next brief spell, when the frozen face of the earth will be upturned, and for another short season be warmed into activity by the sun's embrace.

If one chose, how one could imagine the reviving of hope at every returning summer—the feverish haste of every germ of life to push its growth as soon as the melting snows and softening soil made a move possible. The joyous expectations of the yearlings that the long winter was an exception, and that the return of sunshine heralded a summer which would last all the year! Does that remind you of the song:

> His name yields the richest perfume,
>   And sweeter than music His voice;
> His presence disperses my gloom,
>   And makes all within me rejoice.
> I should, were He always thus nigh,
>   Have nothing to wish or to fear;
> No mortal so happy as I.
>   My summer would last all the year.
>
> Dear Lord, if indeed I am Thine—
>   If Thou art my Sun and my Song,
> Say, why do I languish and pine,
>   And why are my winters so long?
> Oh, drive these dark clouds from my sky,
>   Thy soul-cheering presence restore;
> Then take me to Thee up on high,
>   Where winter and storms are no more.

'Why are my winters so long?' Yes, why? Is it not all a question whether we are turned toward the sun?

Just now it seems to me the devil, by perplexing questions and the fascination of searching after an explanation of deep mysteries, is succeeding too well in drawing the hearts of many toward the cold, dark death of unbelief. To be turned away from God by doubt, makes winter in the soul, which cuts short the growth. Let us hold fast our confidence 'which hath great recompense', and by faith keep our hearts toward God. It can be done, and there never was a time when the living faith of individual hearts was more needed than just now, or when the fruitfulness of abundant spiritual life could be more refreshing to the eyes of the burdened and sinful. And because it is so needed, and might be so fruitful, the devil is striving by every means to make the simple way of faith appear the impossible to some hearts.

I am writing, you will think, almost as though I

thought it were *not* spring with you! It is not that, but I am thinking of those who are in danger from temptations that do press in just now in a special way, and so am rather 'talking out my thoughts' to you. Pray sometimes for such. I think we could be doing more than we know by prayer for each other.

Truly there are mysteries on all sides. I think these days throw a new meaning into the words of the Lord, 'When the Son of man cometh, shall He find faith on the earth?' I do not know; but that there may be faith in me is my daily prayer.

Of all the things I desire for you I would put that first—that your faith might abound. If your heart is drawing near to God in the full assurance of faith, there will be springtime in your world in spite of the devil. A child's simple faith in God's love and faithfulness, and the consequent ordering of life on that assurance, does mean the growth of all that is beautiful, the putting forth of new patience as soon as the patience of past days withers, courage, love, sincerity, abounding more and more. As Paul so clearly puts it, 'the inward man is renewed day by day.' Is not that a good definition of a springtime experience?

The spring is Nature's renewing. Keep your heart turned to the sun, and let no trial or fight or perplexity draw your faith aside; and do inquire sometimes how it fares with those you meet. Some, I know, are struggling; their faith is weak, their winters are long, and it ought not to be so. I believe if we talked more about these things to each other it would be an immense help. There would be less doubting and more faith; less of the season of spiritual inertia, and more of the activity of spring; holiness of heart, and so God's favour and blessing, quickening into life and fruitfulness all the best in us. Do you know those quaint dear lines of Tauler's?

> As the sunflower, ever turning
>   To the mighty sun,
> With the faithfulness of fealty
>   Following only one,
> So make me, Lord, to Thee.

Amen! so make us Lord to Thee through all the changing ways, with their joys and with their sorrows.

Yours, following Jesus still

36

A Birthday Request

My Dear K____,

So you have passed another birthday. I wonder if you feel any older. It is time, I suppose, that you should be grown up in earnest. Anyway, as I used often to feel about you in the Training College, your work and opportunities make demands on you far above your years, and you are rising to meet them.

There are real advantages in being young when you begin God's work; and although I used to think sometimes you were too young, especially as I thought of the sorrowful and more difficult sides of the work, I see how good it is now that you are still quite at the beginning of your own development, and yet also really in the thick of the fight. You see, it means less waste in this sense, that, being actually face to face with the possibilities as well as the difficulties of the life to which you are called, you may set about fitting yourself, knowing what is needed, and leaving out things that, while good enough in themselves, are not necessary to you.

I do want you to be the *best*, the *very best*, for God and the people. This means being the best of which you are capable, for I am more than sure that giving God the best means receiving the best. Many people who have really not had time to think a great deal about themselves as individuals, but who have consistently been giving God their best, will be surprised to find how beautiful they themselves have become. That, partly, is the reason why real saints seldom know that they are saints. It is as though God bestows His beautifying touches on our souls when we are wholly taken up with making something else as good as we know how for Him.

But this is getting rather complicated, and if I go on your eyes will be opening wider and wider, and that look of half-scared bewilderment will be spread over your face as it used to be sometimes in the Training College. It always made me feel 'K____ is a child, and life has surprises for her.'

This is not a birthday letter, because such should be written on or for the day. I did not know about yours till it was past; but thinking of you, and realizing how the time is flying, makes me want to say a few things to you.

You see, K____, I do want the years coming and going to find you growing on the right lines. You were a nice child in the days when I knew you, and you ought to make a true, good woman. I wish you could have been here longer, but that I know so much you have to learn can never be learned here. But just because you were here once, and some lessons came to you here that could not have come otherwise; because I prayed with you and for you, and hoped many things you never knew; because—well, because of many other reasons—I still want to say to you things that you are not obliged to hear as when in the Training College, where I could send for you, and say what I wished.

I want you to be generous. This is the best word I can find to embrace the idea in my mind. Just now we are all facing the inconvenience of shortage in various directions, a shortage that need never have been but for man's own follies and sins. To invite friends to tea has to be considered from the standpoint of rations as well as of desire to have their company.

Lately the College has been so refreshingly bright with wild flowers. I do not know if it is that I have noticed them more, or whether there really have been more; but in so many 'cubes' I see them peering over the edge of some litle mug or other, or out of a saucer full of moss, on the dining-room tables. The other day I found one of the foot-baths literally full of dog-violets getting a refreshing drink before they were distributed. They gave me visions of hedges and woods where there were so many that these violets would hardly be missed.

Yesterday, in the train on my way home to see my sister, I saw the railway banks sprinkled with the gold of the coltsfoot—thousands of blossoms lifting their faces to the sun above the grass.

God seems to me to be trying to teach us a great lesson by the way He has arranged things that are for our own good and our happiness. Unless by our own stupidities we defy His laws, He meets us with such generosity, clearly showing that here is more than we need—how truly more than we deserve! God can always afford to be generous, and so we are rich.

Now you must truly strive to be like the Father in Heaven in His ways of giving, and if you give at all, give generously. Let it be in your life with all the precious things you have to give, that you are able to pour them forth without measuring, just because you have more than enough. It is only when there is a shortage that we have to be rationed!

The dictionary amplifies my word for me and says:

'*Generous*—honourable, bountiful, free to give, courageous as a steed, not meanly.'

What have you to give? Your young heart's love; its faith, its prayers, and its praise. How shall you give? As you will be advised in different ways from time to time—sparingly? As people shall deserve it of you? Think: if you had only received from God what you deserved! Will you give in harmony with the giving of others; or generously, honourably; that is, as you promised, keeping faith with your own heart's intentions? Will you give bountifully—more than people have deserved of you; freely—without thought of getting anything for yourself in return, though you often will, for it is marvellously true that 'with what measure ye mete, it shall be measured to you again'? Will you give courageously; in spite, that is, of other people's sneers or ridicule? To be generous in your opinion or praise of another when some are criticizing and minimizing their work, demands very real courage. Give 'not meanly'; that is, when you have a chance of bestowing your love and care, do it as though there were enough and to spare, not as though you were giving as little as possible.

You are only a little girl, K____, but you could have a large heart, where there should always be a rich, full supply of those precious things all other hearts are deeply needing. Above all, I should like this to be so for you.

I grow so tired of the mean way folk go about God's work. The living water flows in such a little trickle from their hearts. They so seldom seem to have a word of sympathy or encouragement or praise to spare for those about them. It takes a great appeal to bring them to the point of giving. I do not want you to be like that, but this new year, and every year, to find you more large-hearted, more appreciative of others, more glad to give all you have—*more generous*.

Let your thoughtfulness for the happiness of those around you be as plentiful as the coltsfoot on the railway embankment, so that no one will be afraid of calling on you to serve them! Spread abroad the fragrance of your kindly judgment so bountifully that folk may come to count on you to put a good word in for them when no one else is likely to find occasion for one. At this rate, you will be a millionaire so far as heart riches are concerned, for the Scriptures are true: 'There is that scattereth, and yet increaseth.'

May you have many more birthdays, and all spent under the colours! God give you the blessings that are the portion of the generous—special blessings; and scoff the devil out of sight if ever he tempts you to be mean to anyone.

Give! as the morning that flows out of Heaven.
Give! as the waves when their channel is riven;
Give! as the free air and sunshine are given:
   Lavishly, utterly, joyfully give.

You will see this is a new fashion of celebrating a birthday. I make you no gift, but ask you to give instead! May you ever find it 'more blessed'.

37

A MIDNIGHT THOUGHT-JOURNEY

JULY 1917

My Dear N——,

I am sitting in my office. The hour is unearthly, and you are, I hope, sound asleep. All is still, and the quiet after the bustle of the day tempts me to wander by the magic of imagination on a journey of investigation. Where shall I go? You know how to imagine things rather vividly, so I shall ask you to fill in the missing details, and just accompany me on my little excursion.

It is evening. You and X____ have not long returned from the meeting, and you are sitting chatting over the day's happenings while the bread and milk is disposed of, when you hear a sharp knock. Wondering who it can be, you hurry to the door, and after peering for a moment through the dim light to make sure whom you see, you give a little cry as you always used at the Training College, if you were especially pleased or surprised; and, with a real shout to X____, announcing my arrival, you show me into the front room, where, of course, you are living.

Even my imagination fails me when it comes to describing the first few moments. However, before long I have taken off my bonnet, and we are all three sitting at the table. Bread and cheese have been added to the menu, in honour of my presence, and while I eat it I tell you that I have dropped in on you unawares, just to see if you were drinking tea for supper! You are quite indignant at the thought, and immediately plunge into a detailed account of what you eat and drink, and how cleverly you make up tasty bits of the odds and ends that accumulate. While you are telling me this I am looking round for the 'seventeen photos' of yourself, and I catch sight of the little slip which says 'Be not afraid, but speak'; and as you have not stopped talking since I arrived, I am satisfied you have paid attention to the injunction on this occasion.

After a bit you ask me for news of 'our batch', and I tell you that D____ has had a difficult time, but an improvement is showing among the young people. A____ has had a good case of conversion—a man who was got hold of in the pubs. C____ has been a bit troubled with her throat—the air has not suited her; and by the time all my news is given, and the mention of different ones brings up this and that incident, you seem to be suffering from a lump in your throat, and I suggest we take lieutenant up to bed.

So we light the candle, and I set out to inspect her little room. I compliment you both on how nice it is, and notice how well the rigged-up furniture looks. Boxes and a bit of cretonne make quite a pretty dressing table and washstand. The covenant card is fixed so that one could not help seeing it, and there is a flag over the bed-head, besides various other reminders of Training College days and all they represent. You slip off to fix me a bed, while I have a few minutes with X____, and she tells me what a good captain you make, and that she is trying hard to be the sort of lieutenant I described. Then we pray together, and I tell her I shall look in on my way up, to put the light out, in memory of Home Lodge days.

And now I am downstairs again, and you have drawn up the one arm-chair of which your quarters boast. And having seated yourself opposite to me on a little three-legged stool, we are talking. Even this unearthly hour cannot make my imagination vivid enough to tell me just what you are saying in answer to my questions, though I know well enough the sort of things I should be saying to you; but as you read this letter you can easily fill in your part, and thus have the complete account.

First, I want to know all about the corps, how you feel now you have settled in to know the people. Some things have been more difficult than you expected; but, in spite of that, are you honestly endeavouring to carry out the ideals you set out with? Are you able to work by the regulations? And what about the things we have so often discussed one way or another—using your soldiers; visiting the outsiders; the workhouse; varying the form of meetings and open-airs. What about the wind-up collection, and going out to meals, and shopping in a wollen cap, or a plain hat?

We have a good laugh over some things, for I can imagine you would have interesting bits to tell me, and we both get excited when it comes to the story of the woman who was in the 'pub' the first Saturday you went; and as to the boys who have lately got saved—well, you are so full of it that it is not long before I am fully convinced you will shortly have a young people's band; and you finish by asking me if I will come and present the instruments. You do not know a bit where they are coming from, but that is a detail!

Well, and then I ask about your health and spirits. Are you wise with your food? I try to impress you again with the importance of keeping fit, and threaten to give you a mustard pack just to remind you of what it feels like! That makes you remember a success you have had nursing an old woman, and you tell me all about her, and how you have now made one of your corps cadets responsible for looking after her regularly for you.

Soon, of course, I am asking you about yourself. What news have you from your own people? What books are you reading? Then, are you keeping good? After so long in the field are you still fully saved? Have you really proved the power of the Lord to keep you wholly His? Is the Blessing still the crowning possession of your life?

You have temptations and strangely unexpected difficulties, and as I write I long to be really with you so that you might have, at any rate, the comfort of talking your side of things out. That cannot be, but, oh, I *do* pray, N____, that you may really talk to the Lord. If I were talking to you actually, I know I should say: 'Talk more and more to God as you would to some loved and trusted one. Pray not merely in the sense of asking for something—but talk out your feelings and perplexities, your own, and those that are yours because they are those of the people who are yours. Commune with God about them; that is, explain, seek, ask, spread them before Him.'

There is great joy in my heart at the thought of you. I count on you and trust you, as well as pray and believe for you. You are standing up for Jesus before the people of your district. I know you meant it when you used to sing here:

> I'll stand for Christ, for Christ alone,
>   Amid the tempest and the storm.
> Where Jesus leads I'll follow on,
>   I'll stand for Christ alone.

And I love to think you are actually putting it into practice, not slackening one scrap for the difficulty, but rather being the more resolute.

Well, I am growing sleepy, and it would be wisest to stop writing, unless, having seen you so vividly in imagination, I might be thinking I saw the door opening; or, whether it opened or not, I might think I saw you coming in! So I finish my thought-journey with the picture of you and me kneeling together in your little room. I wish I knew what it was really like. And we are praying as we have often prayed; and for the time it does not seem to me as if you are really gone from me, and turned into an officer, but as though you were still my cadet whom the Lord gave me to help to look after, for a bit, and so to pray with you is my right.

But it is only imagination after all; and instead of writing more, I shall stop and make a real finish to the letter by kneeling here for a little time in the quiet hour, and asking the Lord Jesus to bless and keep you, to give you a good time among your folk; and, above all, to keep your spirit simple, sincere, and earnest, and help you to do the Salvation Army morning, noon, and night, and that in every fight you may 'see the tempter fly'!

I shall be hoping, too, that one of these days I may hear a knock in reality and find that you have come in to see me, which will be next best to my coming to see you. There is a song, isn't there, with a line that says something about: 'And to Canaan we'll return by and by.' Well, you might return to the Training College by and by, just for a visit!

I told Colonel I should be writing, and she sent you her love, and said I was to tell you that, at all cost, you must keep the spirit of loving and caring and serving—which is the Spirit of God and of the Salvation Army; and then all will be well. So it will! God keep you!

38

ON KEEPING UP THE STANDARD

AUGUST 1917

My Dear M_____,

When you were on furlough I had hoped to be able to arrange a further talk together. There are many things in my heart that I should like to say to you, things that could be more easily said than written. But it may be long before I have the opportunity of speaking to you again, so I send this letter.

If, when you receive it, you are in a hurry, or particularly anxious about something, or not in the mood to be talked to seriously, put this by, and at some other time—perhaps in the quiet of the late evening when your own spirit is more still, and daily things less insistent—give some thought to this letter and its subject.

You are still young, and at that place in your life where few things can touch you lightly. Your impressionable nature makes it easy to affect you, so to speak, out of proportion to the facts. You do not feel by halves, and have not yet learnt how to throw things off; so you suffer and rejoice not always in fair measure.

Some learn the secret of keeping the characteristics of youth long after youth has passed. On the whole, I believe such people are the richest in the experiences that make life wonderful and beautiful; but they find also, perhaps, more tears and burdens.

I cannot tell how it will be with you. Sometimes when I pray I am torn between two longings for those I love—that the loved should travel by easy ways, and that the deepest joys of life should come to them. Both prayers, it seems to me, cannot be answered in the same life.

Whether the child in you will survive the years, I do not know; but I do know that just now there is certainly no doubt that enough of the child remains to make you capable of finding transcendent joy and tragic grief in the things of every day; and it is because you are still so open to influences from men and things, that I want to say a little to you about yourself.

I want you to see there is reason to hope for good things from the fact that you are still open to impressions. The best can still affect you. You are not set hard in a mould. This makes my joy, if also my anxiety, where you are concerned; my hope and my fear. If only I knew how to protect you from every evil influence, and bring you into contact only with ennobling things! I do not. I can only pray for you, and try to make you understand a little better how to protect yourself from anything hurtful, and keep your heart open to receive all good.

I know that you do not agree with me on some points, but I do want you to be one with me in the belief, the unshakable belief, that nothing can really influence you against your will.

I feel that if you thoroughly accept this, it will, on the one hand, help you to rise up and fight with the courage of hope to maintain the high ideal your spirit has conceived against anything that could spoil it; and, on the other hand, to do away at one sweep with the whole array of excuses the devil has prepared for your use.

The attacks of evil against the soul wholly given up to God are seldom straightforward, and just at this time you are, I think, faced with one of the most subtle of such. If you triumph, the strength of victory will remain with you for ever. If you are overcome, some of your highest ambitions, and the best hopes of others for you, will never be realized.

You set forth, not so long ago, cherishing high ideals, generous feelings overflowing your heart, your spirit burning with zeal to sacrifice and suffer for the Kingdom of Christ. To change this is the devil's aim. Is he succeeding?

The weapon against you is two-edged. First you are to be deceived into thinking all have gone back from 'the highway'. The faithful are no longer to be found in the land! Your heart is made sick with disappointment because of the things you see and hear; the way you are treated! The standard apparently accepted by the majority of those to whom you had looked expectantly for help is so different from what you had set up! The first result of all this is to bring you into an atmosphere of isolation that makes your spirit tremble as under the weight of a great burden.

You are willing to fight, to suffer, to sacrifice, but you have associated it with the helpful comradeship of kindred spirits. You know you are not cut out to live apart from your fellows. You long to share your joys and struggles with one of like spirit. While you are perplexed and hesitating, circumstances conspire to invite your censure of the actions of others. From condemnation of their faults you pass to bitterness and disloyalty, and so your own spirit is injured.

To your own heart there follows the suggestion that your standard is too high. Practical experience shows you, and the example of others proves, that it was a mistake, a dream, a visionary impossibility; and the happiest and easiest way is to relinquish your hold and sink down to the level of the obtainable. So that you be as good as others, why bother?

I felt when you were speaking to me that either you have already yielded to the subtle insinuations or are now on the point of giving up some of the things you meant should always be your possession. That capacity to receive quickly and be influenced greatly by impressions from without was given that your spirit should be stirred by every high, inspired by every noble thing; your heart ready to leap in response to the call, whether to follow some great example or to meet some deep need. These days of youth, days of quick impressions, of swift sorrows and high happiness, were meant to be, above all, days of growth. Lowering the standard? No; raising it! Losing sight of the ideal? No; drawing near to complete the perfect details! But you see how the very capacity for this involves capacity for the opposite—susceptibility to evil influences. So the devil works.

I long to see him defeated by you. He lies. Do not believe any human conception of goodness could be better than goodness, and yet be false. If it be good, it is true, and by the help of Jesus attainable. Know, once and for ever, that unless you, your own self, are as good as you see you ought to be, you are not fulfilling your destiny.

As I write I have been praying. I see you, M——, as you could be, and my heart is moved. You must—surely you will—rise above the machinations of evil, and be what God has made you capable of being! These are for you days when habit of thought is hardening into character. If only now you can keep your heart pure, your mind humble, your spirit self-renouncing, you will grow up before God in the likeness of His Son, and the world in which you dwell shall know it.

I come back to what I said: *you cannot be influenced against your will*. Let it be your will to keep your heart open to every good, and closed to every evil influence; your face turned toward the sun, away from the shadow.

Love the true. Walk, act, speak, think the truth. Despise the lie wherever you find it, however well disguised, however advantageous the point at which it promises to bring you out: short cuts to a desired end which necessitate a deviation from the way of truth involve you in unknown dangers; and, even if they were safe, they degrade the soul that travels them.

Show mercy. No soul was ever made poor by loving too much, or injured by forgiving too often; and many, very many, have found the reward so wonderful that places in life have seemed to be part of Heaven. *Scorn selfishness*. Steel your spirit against every influence that could incline you to seek things for yourself—you are given for others; against jealousy, it comes from Hell, and will make Hell in your heart; yes, even the least little bit of it; loathe it; against pride, it is born of selfishness and makes people fools and blind.

I am in the country, rested by the sight of the fields and flowers—flowers so various in beauty that they seem to me a demonstration of the vastness of the Mind that imagined them. But I see each spring up 'after his kind'. The wild rose can only be a wild rose, a thistle for evermore a thistle; to man only, God gave the power to change his way. To you He gives it, and with it comes the responsibility to use it.

I want you to choose well, to open your heart only to the influences that lift. I like to think of you with your face towards the highway. And why should it not be so? Except inasmuch as you may help them, leave other people to decide the standard of conduct by which they are content to be governed; for yourself, be content with nothing less than the best you know. In the world of the spirit the humblest may strive after the highest with hope of success, for you will not be alone; there is One who will work with you.

This letter does not, I find, express all I meant to say, but I pray it may help you to think things out for yourself.

God bless you!

39
DOG-VIOLETS AND 'DOG-OFFICERS'

NOVEMBER 1917

My Dear B____,

I am going to tell you a few things I have heard lately. Things we hear are often not worth taking notice of, and folk who form their opinions by what 'they say' seldom have opinions worth taking into account. At the same time, we do sometimes discover facts by listening with discretion.

Not long ago a parcel reached me in which I found several sprays of red berries, a few purple and gold blackberry leaves, and, wrapped in cool, green moss, a few dog-violet roots, bearing, in spite of the autumn days, several very self-possessed looking blooms. They *were* lovely, and I wished, as I had often done before, that they had a scent as sweet as their looks. I began to wonder why they had not.

If you have a very strong imagination—you remember we used to say in field drill class that every one has the capacity, but some need to cultivate it—well, if you have a vivid imagination, you will understand how it was that the moss answered my wonderings. Moss does not often give information on any subject, being for the most part far too busy keeping itself fresh and green as it creeps, beautifying quietly every unsightly object it can reach; but it has a great store of information, and is always worth hearing, if only because of the long way its memory can go back. And so I heard it say:

'The violet thou namest "dog" cometh of the same family as the one thou namest "sweet", and in past times was of equal sweetness; but in an evil day a certain young violet reasoned within himself asking, "Why should I diffuse fragrance that addeth no whit to my beauty or comfort, ministering by it only to the pleasure of plants and creatures about me, some of which indeed have not even the capacity to appreciate the sweetness I pour out? Let us try," he continued, addressing those of his family within hearing, "whether we may not grow as well, and be as much admired, and yet save ourselves the effort of bestowing fragrance on all with whom we have to do. At least, let it be given only where we see it may help to bring us some gain, or in the presence of the very high."

'Soon they found how well they might still look in the eyes of all who saw them from afar. Indeed, they seemed to grow in beauty, all their efforts being put forth in that direction. The delicate lines were more clearly pencilled, the shades of blue more varied; they even learned to lift their faces and look over the heads of their neighbours. The birds darting past called to each other to notice how blue the violets were this spring, but, having no word to say to them, never missed the sweet scent. As with the birds, so with many strangers who beheld from a distance the vivid petals.

'From time to time, as they needed some service from others, the sweet perfume would again fill the air; but by degrees they either lost the power to produce it or were too much taken up with themselves to think of pleasing their neighbours by showing either gratitude or respect in the old way.

'So it was that there grew violets without the delicate fragrance which in the past had made all dealings with them so pleasant even to their humblest acquaintances.

'Also,' the moss added—for, being very ancient, he carried strange notions in his mind—'thou shouldest know there is a fragrance spread by man, making his dealings with his fellows pleasant. As with the violets, it is a thing not seen nor heard, adding no beauty that a stranger may observe from afar, but making itself felt at once by all who come near. It hath many names, and is perhaps of different degrees in different men, as the fragrance of one flower differeth from another. Some would name it gratitude, some courtesy, and others respect. The man shedding it about him is called, properly, gentleman; the same signifying, not his possession in outward place or prospect, but that gentle spirit that addeth a fragrance to all words and deeds.'

So I listened, and, tucking the violets in among the moss in a saucer, wondered if they understood how a sweet scent shed abroad would have been in them the touch of perfection.

And this I heard, too. A brigade of new cadets marching smartly down Linscott Road was met by a brigadier whose white hair waved under her bonnet, telling in its silent way of long years of joyful sacrifice and loving service; but only three of the cadets returned her salute.

Again I heard. A young lieutenant, helpful to a faithful warrior entering her twentieth year of service for God and souls, spoke of her in thoughtless disrespect as 'the old lady'.

Again I hear of crowded meetings. A soldier of Christ proclaiming His message, who has been doing it since before the birth of the two young officers appointed to assist; but they stroll in late for two meetings out of three on that Sunday.

And still again, of reproof given by one of long experience and advanced age, and in place of the expression of regret and assurance of improvement there is something very like resentment, excuse, and the showing of an 'uppish' spirit.

I hear of business long delayed through unanswered letters; of services rendered, but no thanks given; of ill health and weariness, and no expression of comradely solicitude or sympathy. I hear, in short, of the dog-violet—'dog-officer' well dressed, well developed, well thought of by those at a distance, but lacking the fragrance of gratitude and respect and kindliness, and thus robbed of the charm they might so easily diffuse. Many a comrade is lonely and discouraged, and many a leader burdened and depressed, who might have been cheered, comforted, and blessed by the kind of fragrance I mean.

The salute betokening mutual respect and greeting given in the passing moment; evidences of thought for comrades older than ourselves, whatever their rank; readiness to accept correction without giving expression to hasty annoyance, often bordering on rudeness—all these and other expressions of the 'right spirit' might help to make life so much more pleasant for all with whom we come in contact. And how easily this fragrance might be shed abroad by all of us who are proud to call ourselves officers in the Army!

What do you think, B____? I do not know if you ever wished dog-violets were sweet, or if you ever had to do with a comrade whose spirit you wished had been fragrant. Whether or not, take care not to make the mistake the dog-violets made, by coming to the conclusion that fragrance does not matter. It *does* matter, and there is all too little of it in the world just now. So be resolved to spread it around all you can.

Yours, believing that your life
shall be fragrant always

40

THE LAW OF THE FOREST

DECEMBER 1917

My Dear D____,

You were, I remember, even in the first days of our acquaintance, interested in all manner of writings, and fond of tracing a line of thought through the jungle of words in which it seemed hidden.

It is long since we had any opportunity for discussion on such lines, but thinking it may interest you, I send a 'writing', wondering if in some spare moment you will find time to look through it, and then perhaps amuse yourself by trying to trace a deeper meaning than lies on the surface. At least it will occasion an exercise of thought on your part, and that will not be useless; real thinking never is.

There had been a storm—wind and rain beating down— and the trees on the edge of the copse had borne the full force of the gale as it swept in from the sea and over the heather-covered common, without meeting any obstacle to turn aside or lessen its fury. Now, though the sun shone, the clouds were still driving hurriedly across the deep blue of the heavens, and from the denser banks assembled to windward it was easy to anticipate a renewal of the storm.

In spite of these distant threatenings, the spot where I sat sheltered from the wind by the thick undergrowth was full of enchantment; and behind me in the wood I could hear the wind sighing, singing, sometimes shouting, as it surged through the tree tops. Do you know the sound of it—the particular sound if most of the trees are pines? When it swelled in volume, the trees bent and swayed, and the root on which I sat felt like a great muscle rising as it tightened to resist the pull.

At the time, nothing unusual impressed itself upon my mind, but later I found myself possessed of a knowledge which certainly was, to say the least, unlooked for. Had a subconscious impression drawn out and quickened some dormant sense, making secrets known, but leaving no explanation in my mind as to how I came by them? I cannot tell; but the experience being clear to my mind I am recording it, so that should there be a recurrence thereof, I might compare the later impression with the first, and who knows but that some meaning might evolve?

I seemed to know that long, long ago the wind was sighing in the branches just as I had heard it, when, toward evening, during a lull of an hour or so, a tall, well-grown pine, standing on the outskirts of the wood, bowed its glorious brow of branches and said, 'How long?' Whether there were any who understood the question or who knew the answer, I cannot say. There was no reply. Again there was a movement, and the pine threw out its wide arms toward the glow in the west and sighed, 'How long?'

I thought I heard a low murmur of voices replying on all sides, 'Until the service is completed.' In this I may be mistaken, for without reference to the words, the pine tree presently continued: 'How long shall I stand here open to the buffets of every wind that blows'—and then I noticed its well-grown head reared above its fellows, so that in truth all winds would reach it—'labouring day and night in secret, that my roots may grow quickly enough to stand the strain? How long shall I grow for the comfort of birds who expect me to bear their nests, and who seldom seem grateful even when I risk cracking rather than expose them to the full force of the spring winds? How long shall I spread my branches wider, and always be asked to spread them wider still, that there may be shelter from the sun for the beasts who dwell on the common, and who seem to think I was planted for no other purpose than to cool their backs? How long shall the frivolous and empty-headed squirrel make a convenience of me to hoard his foolish little treasures? How long?

The gamekeeper's gun was right, little as I thought it, when he leaned against my trunk that morning years ago, and told me I should go on making a convenience of myself for others until I was old and rotten; whereas I might, if I would, be carried out of the forest, and honoured, polished, and valued; instead of caring, be cared for; instead of sheltering, be sheltered; instead of being merely rough and upright, as one must be in a forest where there are storms to meet, be shaped with elegance and admired by those whose opinion was____'

The last sentences had been difficult to catch, for the wind was rising steadily, and the final words were drowned by the thunder of sound that swept up the hillside, and broke into a thousand notes among the trees.

As the morning sun peered over the stretches of common and his rays crept forward, to touch with gold the wonderful red stem and twisted branches of the great pine at the edge of the wood, they faded with astonishment into the dark undergrowth beyond; for the tree had fallen! The violence of the storm scarcely accounted for such a downfall. Longer and fiercer gales had shaken the wood, and there had been no fear that the trees would yield. No other tree had fallen, though there were younger and older, and many not as strong, as this well-balanced, deeply-rooted giant.

Through the days that followed there was wonder and grief in the hearts of many weak and trustful creatures. The squirrels, chattering and quarrelsome, but still lovable, trembled as they crept about the prostrate branches. The birds flitted uneasily to and fro, especially the young whose first world had been those wondrous rocking boughs. Older, nobler birds, who had looked from year to year for the same spot in which to trust their young, now circled over it in anxious surprise. The mild-eyed heifers wandered up, and stood gazing as if they saw past the tree to its furthest future, and then turned wearily aside, for when the sun was high no other trees stretched their branches far enough beyond the hedge that encircled the wood to afford the denizens of the outer world shelter.

Whether the tree itself had any knowledge of all this, I know not. It gave no sign, and in due course was taken away, leaving an emptiness where it had stood, and crushed and broken fronds and tendrils where it had lain.

Through the autumn weeks a deep silence rested over the wood. Even the squirrels skipped less than usual, and went on with their gossiping and quarrelling in a more subdued fashion. In the immediate vicinity of the tree, a thousand small creatures had been destroyed by its fall, and thousands more had lost their home and shelter. How many little hopes crushed out and how many fears created, none could say. All night there might be noticed a sighing among the pines. Later there broke forth a murmuring of anxious questioning, as the trees discussed together whether the fallen comrade had been justified, and if so, could they still be content with the life of the woods? Yet, to break away from their roots____!

One still night when the questioning was more earnest than before, the ancient oak in the centre of the wood shook off the remnant of its summer leaf, and from its bold old heart, spoke. The anxious pines listened, still and silent, but eager to hear. He spoke of the ancient laws governing all noble forests; of the privilege of trees planted in companies to share the strain of the storm and uphold each other; of the duty of every tree that sprang from roots to hold to those roots, to strengthen and deepen them. He shows how life came from them; how strength to stand upright and bear wide branches depended on them; that to break from them meant to lose the sap of life.

In quiet tones he passed on to tell of the great purpose for which such effort should be put forth; not only that the trees might grow strong and beautiful, but, more than all, that every living creature who trusted to them for protection or nourishment might never be disappointed.

He mentioned by name many of the inhabitants of the wood, and showed how great a thing it was to stand from year to year as an abiding home for these. He spoke of those who might come from afar to find shelter or safety, and of how it should be his and their pride and joy to be found always there. The glory of the tree, he said, should be to give shelter rather than to receive it; to protect, even while it stood unprotected; to nourish, to uphold, to grow upright and strong, to hold to its roots in every storm for the comfort of all other creatures, 'until' as expressed by the ancient motto of the forest trees, which he reminded them had been handed down by the elders to every seedling in its first years, 'the service is completed.' Of the brother who fell he said only, that in his strength he had departed from the first law, and had begun to think about himself before the service was completed.

After he had ceased, there was silence for a long space. The next night the first storm of winter rode over land and sea, and later in the day a bird fought its way toward the wood, tossed hither and thither by the wind. With one last effort it beat its rain-soaked wings to the spot where the great branches had once stretched out toward the bleak spaces of the common, and in the fading light of the winter day sank down exhausted to the cold, wet earth to die. The sheltering boughs on which its last hope counted were not there.

From that night roots were more firmly held, branches more widely stretched, and before long a seedling was being instructed how to grow in that spot so unexpectedly made vacant. It grew and grew, and always with the ambition to live according to the law of the great forest trees to which family it belonged, and until the service should be completed.

I made it clear at the beginning of this account that I do not know how this knowledge came to me. I do not know either how it was that just as clearly as in my mind I can picture the tree on the edge of the wood by the common, on whose root I sat listening to the wind in the branches, so clearly do I know that this was the tree which grew up to fill the vacant place. The tree is real enough, and I could take you to it, but as for the rest____!

This is the 'writing'. Can you make anything of it, and would you consider the following quotations have any bearing on it?

'I will plant in the wilderness the cedar, I will set in the desert the fir tree and the pine.'

'A cedar in Lebanon with fair branches, and with a shadowing shroud, and of an high stature; and his top was among the thick boughs.'

'Therefore his height was exalted above all the trees of the field, and his boughs were multiplied, and his branches became long, because of the multitude of waters.'

'All the fowls of heaven made their nests in his boughs, and under his branches did all the beasts of the field bring forth their young.

'Thus was he fair in his greatness, in the length of his branches: for his root was by great waters.'

'Blessed is the man that trusteth in the Lord, and whose hope the Lord is. For he shall be as a tree planted by the waters, and that spreadeth out her roots.'

'That they might be called trees of righteousness, the planting of the Lord, that He might be glorified.'

If you find an interpretation, write and tell me; but at least we might both appropriate the words 'until the service is completed'. And that recalls me to the fact that unless I hurry up, much of today's share will *not* be completed!

Yours, serving

41
FAREWELL WORDS

JANUARY 1918

And so, My Dear Girls,

There are to be no more monthly Training College letters to you—at least, not from me. The editor has kindly allowed me this opportunity of sending you a closing word—a kind of postscript, I suppose, it might be called.

I have not actually left the old place, and am writing this in my own room at the Lodge. I cannot help it that my mind keeps slipping back to another day when, in a foreign land, I sat in a little wooden châlet by the bedside of my brave little sister Miriam, writing the first letter to you through the medium of 'The Officer'. When she roused from her rest I read it over to her, and she helped me by her criticism and suggestion. Now I am writing this last one, which she will never see, for we shall lay her dear body to rest on the day when this is posted to the editor.

All is telling me that a period of my life is passed. This incomparable change in our home circle, the break with the work that bound me to so many of you, and the closing of these openings of the heart and mind, which have been used by the Lord to help some of you, I know—perhaps more than I know.

When parting messages are given, it does not so much matter whether the same things have been said before, as that what we want to say be said. I want to say that, while it is quite true that writing you has often been a burden in the sense that it has been difficult to find time, and more difficult still to express what seemed likely to be any good to you, it has been ever a joy to know that the letter was a little thing I could still do for love of you— something I was not exactly obliged to do—something that meant a little giving for your sakes, in a way you will never know. There is always joy in giving when the heart wants to give, and I should like you all to know and believe that my heart has longed to do for you more, far more, than I could ever actually accomplish.

Perhaps I may still find some ways of serving you. I shall search for them as for treasures, and be careful not to waste any I find, but with love and prayer use each as wisely as I can.

The point of what I am trying to say is this: *it has been and will be a joy to do anything for any of you*. I am going from the Training College, and there will be no more cadets who are mine; but that, I think, makes all the old ones the more mine. Will you think it too? For, as I was writing to one of you the other day: 'No changes of seasons or place could make any change in my mind' so far as helping you is concerned.

I want to say, also, that I do believe in you and in your opportunity. Dear girls, it was never more worth while being and doing the best for the world than now; and you are the people to be and do, through God, such things as shall be worthy of the highest traditions of the Army. Will you have more faith for yourselves and more courage in dealing with your own hearts' fears and feelings?

Often my heart hurts with the aching to do more to help my father, our General. I see him so burdened with anxieties, and responsibilities, spending all of heart and mind and body for the Army and all for which it stands. Could not we younger officers cheer his heart by such a rising up to do and dare, as should give an impetus, not only to those in our own immediate surroundings, but as should spread on all sides in holy inspiration and devotion. Why not?

I want to ask you once more, quite frankly and plainly, if you have kept, and do now live in, the Blessing of Holiness? Is the assurance of it hidden in your heart? Are the beautiful tokens of it so manifest in your life that those with whom you live and work know it too? This living Christ's life is the 'one thing needful'. Rank, position, work, health, happiness, love, are all in a degree precious, but all nothing if the heart is not clean. How is it with you?

May I say to one: If all is not clear in your own experience, as it once was; if there have crept in doubts, selfishness, worldliness; will you now *resolve* that there shall begin a search after Him that shall only be satisfied when your soul is by His Presence cleansed again, purified as by fire, sanctified for a service which knows no limitations but those of time and strength, and no ambitions but for His glory? Will you?

Pray for Colonel. While she is in the 'old place' it will represent to us the standard of zeal and devotion. She has been an example that shall endure for ever, and we love her for it.

'Little children, it is the last time . . . I have not written unto you because ye know not the truth, but because ye know it, and that no lie is of the truth . . . Let that therefore abide in you, which ye have heard from the beginning. If that which ye have heard from the beginning shall remain in you, ye also shall continue in the Son, and in the Father. And now, little children, abide in Him; that, when He shall appear, we may have confidence, and not be ashamed before Him at His coming.'

'And not be ashamed!' Oh, may the Holy Spirit so help us now that for you, for me, in the small things, in the hidden thoughts, there shall be nothing of which to be ashamed before Him. May the Lord Jesus be with us, guiding, strengthening, and keeping, all according to His will.

Lord Jesus, Thou dost keep Thy child
  Through sunshine or through tempests wild;
Jesus, I trust in Thee.
  Thine is such wondrous power to save;
Thine is the mighty love that gave
  Its all on Calvary.

Love perfecteth what it begins;
  Thy power doth save me from my sins:
Thy grace upholdeth me.
  This life of trust, how glad, how sweet!
My need and Thy great fullness meet,
  And I have all in Thee.

Yours, for God and the Army to the end,
Catherine Booth

EXPLANATORY NOTES

Terms used in the Salvation Army and Training College

Blessing, the The Salvation Army teaches that conversion should lead to the deeper blessing of full commitment to Christ, demonstrated in holy living, or sanctification.

Boomers 'Salvationists' who sell Army publications, such as *The War Cry*.

Brigade A group of cadets, in the care of a sergeant.

Cadet Student at The Salvation Army training college for officers.

Commissioning time Climax of open session, when cadets are commissioned as officers and appointed to their first Army post.

Corps Local branch of The Salvation Army – local church.

Corps cadets Very young people in the corps wanting to get training to serve The Army.

Covenant day The last 'spiritual day' before session ended, when new officers signed a card setting out their covenant of loyalty to God and the Army.

'Cubes' Cubicles or tiny bedroom for cadets at the training college.

DC Divisional Commander, officer equivalent to a bishop, in charge of all the corps in his area.

DHQ Divisional Headquarters – administrative offices of DC.

Field Drill Class Classes at which cadets were taught how to lead open-air and indoor meetings and other evangelistic enterprises.

FO Field Officer – officer in charge of a local corps (i.e. church).

Furlough Officer's leave – three weeks a year (they worked a seven-day week with no evenings off!).

'Half hour', the Half an hour a day set aside for cadets to meditate and pray.

Hallelujah lassies Young women first billed as 'Hallelujah lasses' in Gateshead before The Christian Mission became The Salvation Army. It was regarded as a more attractive term than 'lady preacher' or 'singer'. The name stuck.

Holiness meetings Meetings at which the Salvation Army doctrine of sanctification or holiness of life for the believer, was taught.

Home Lodge House adjoining the Training Garrison, where Catherine Bramwell-Booth lived and took batches of Cadets for a month, to give them more personal supervision and care.

Hydro Hydropathy, or treatment of illness with hot and cold water, practised by the Booth family and at first taught to officers.

Officer A Salvationist trained and committed to full-time service for The Army for life.

Peddling Salvation Army 'peddlers' sold goods, often made in their social institutions, to help funds.

Penitent form - or Mercy seat Wooden bench at the front of an Army hall, where those wanting to find Christ or to renew consecration come to kneel.

'Personal', a A personal interview of the cadet by a member of training college staff.

Pinning on ribbon Small piece of Army tricolour ribbon pinned to the chest of a new convert to help him witness to his new faith.

Quarters Officer's lodgings.

Recruits Converts wishing to become soldiers, under instruction.

Regulations Army guidelines for corps officers, officers, soldiers, etc.

Ribbon A narrow strip of ribbon of the Army colours – yellow, red and blue – which was pinned onto the new convert.

Roll Official list of all Salvationists enrolled in a particular corps.

SD Self-denial week, held annually, to give and collect money for the work.

Shelter Salvation Army hostel for vagrants or destitute people.

Side classes Devotional meetings for the women's side or men's side of cadet training.

Soldiers Converts, over fourteen, received into Army membership at their local corps.

Spiritual Day Held one Tuesday a month, during training, when the General or Chief of Staff (his next-in-command) would speak to cadets.

Testimony Every new convert was encouraged to 'give his testimony' – tell publicly, soon after conversion, what God had done for him.

Training Garrison Training college for officer cadets, originally at the Congress Hall in Linscott Road, Clapton, London.

YPS-M Young people's sergeant major, local officer in charge of children's work in the local corps.